UNDERSTANDING PREPOSITIONS

BY KEVIN KIRK

THIS BOOK BELONGS TO

Published by Indgenius Limited
61 Bridge Street, Kington, Herefordshire, HR5 3DJ, UK

This book forms part of the CORE English series, see the website for details: **www.englishbook.shop**

Quantity sales. Special discounts are available on quantity purchases by corporations, associations, libraries, schools and others. Members of the website also qualify for discounts. Please see the website for details.

UNDERSTANDING PREPOSITIONS
Written by Kevin Kirk
A CORE English Reference Book
1st Edition
First Published in 2019

ISBN 978-1-9160757-1-9

E&OE

ACKNOWLEDGEMENTS

This book is dedicated to the memory of Peter Kirk who died, aged 19, from diabetes related complications. Peter helped enormously in the initial stages of the creation of the CORE series. He compiled the phrasal verb and idiom lists and wrote most of the definitions and examples. He also provided many of the sample sentences in the noun and adjective books.

He is sorely missed.

It is also dedicated to my mum, without whom I wouldn't have been here to write it.

REWARD

Is the copy of the book you are holding genuine? Does it have a distinctive watermark on the reference pages? If not it might be an unauthorised copy. This book took 1,000s of hours to produce and just copying it is not only not fair but will force the price up for honest people like you. If you suspect this copy isn't real then please contact us via the website and you can be eligible for a reward.

www.englishbook.shop/copying

CONTENTS

CONTENTS

CONTENTS

CONTENTS

WHAT IS CORE ENGLISH?

CORE English is a methodology that was designed to make it easier for English language students to visualize how the language fits together in order to create grammatically correct sentences. In doing so it overturns, or modifies, a certain number of established grammatical 'rules'. It was based on over 7 years of research undertaken at Mahidol University in Thailand and was developed with the help and cooperation of over 2,000 students of varying abilities. The word CORE doesn't represent either an adjective or a noun, but, instead, it represents a verb as it basically cuts out certain sections of a sentence based on the central focus (i.e. the core) in order to study or modify them. In order to demonstrate the methodology in simple terms let us look at a particular sentence construct and how it is being taught at present:

In the afternoon a small number of the more health conscious students will be exercising.

Ok, so let's break that down into the constituent parts of speech:

In	Preposition
the	Definite article
afternoon	Noun
a	Indefinite article
small	Adjective
number	Noun
of	Preposition
the	Definite article
more	Comparative adjective
health	Noun
conscious	Adjective
students	Plural Noun
will	Modal Verb
be	Auxiliary verb
exercising	Present participle of the verb 'exercise'

Imagine being a learner and being confronted with that. When teaching a sentence construct like this you'd normally start with something simpler:

Today the students exercise.

Word	Type
Today	Adverb
the	Article/Determiner
students	Noun
exercise	Verb (Intransitive)

Now, what about if we used this same construct with the sentence on the previous page?

Word Cluster	Type
In the afternoon	Adverb
a small number of the	Article/Determiner
more health conscious students	Noun
will be exercising	Verb (Intransitive)

This, in essence, is what CORE is all about. It 'clumps' word clusters into types, which then become interchangeable. So, a beginner can start off with simple constructs and simply substitute more complex structures to add granularity and nuance to what they are trying to say.

Adverb: the above representation is a prepositional phrase, these are used to add granularity to where something appears in time or space. If we use the simple adverb, **today**, it gives us a broad idea of when something is taking place, but we may need to have more details, for example we may want to attend, so we use prepositional phrases. For example: **today** may be represented by the prepositional phrase **in the afternoon** and if we want to add even more granularity we simply add another prepositional phrase to indicate the start time, **from 2 p.m.** and we can also add an end time using another preposition phrase, **to 4 p.m.** So **today** and **in the afternoon from 2 p.m. to 4 p.m.** are interchangeable and can both be regarded as adverbs.

                    Website: www.englishbook.shop

Article/Determiner: articles and determiners are usually regarded as special types of adjectives and, for the most part, are single use words that each have to be learned separately. In CORE they are treated as a special grammatical type and range from single words (like a, an, the, some or any) through to complex clusters consisting of various word types. Each cluster conveys a special meaning so the learner can move from the simple **the** (indicating a specific group) to **a small number of the** (indicating a particular subset of a specific group).

Noun: In most EFL classes we focus on the specific word(s) that attach a description (or label) to something, such that it can be recognised. In CORE this definition is broadened out using adjectives, so that nouns can be represented by noun phrases (as in the example above) or even adding verbs and adverbs so, what we consider to be noun clauses, are treated as simple nouns in terms of sentence construction. So the simple **students** could be replaced by the phrase, **more health conscious students** or a noun clause like **students who want to keep fit.** Grammar 'purists' would say that the noun clause example here is actually a noun (**students**) plus an adjective clause (**who want to keep fit**) but it is essentially interchangeable with a noun; so, in CORE it is regarded as a noun.

Verb: In CORE, verbs are regarded as single entities, so the simple bare infinitive verb **exercise** could be exchanged with a more complex structure, such as **will be exercising**, depending on the context. So all the learner has to do is to choose the action/state and then choose the tense/voice using the context.

To summarize, in CORE grammatical terms the following sentences have the same construct and elements within them and can be freely interchanged.

Today	the	students	exercise
⇕	⇕	⇕	⇕
In the afternoon from 2 p.m to 4 p.m	a small number of the	more health conscious students	will be exercising

TYPE CONSTRUCTS

Some of the grammatical constructs in the methodology are fairly rigid and unchanging, others are infinitely variable. The main constructs are:

Adverbs (variable): single word adverbs basically consist of 4 basic types (plus adjective graduators and conjunctions), which can vary in terms of sentence position. These words are generally used to describe things like methods or positions in time or space. To these single words you must add the extremely variable (and flexible) prepositional phrases, which can add granularity to how, where or when something exists or has been done, how it was done and by how much.

Articles and Determiners (fixed): These constructs follow a predictable pattern, with the exception of some optional adjective graduators, so you can merely study the various definitions and choose the one that best suits your context using the reference book.

Nouns (variable): Nouns are primarily labels and have to be learned in order to recognise objects or entities (they are generally the first things we learn when we learn a language). Nouns are unique to every person and, in general, the larger the number of nouns the person knows the better their range of English. On the other hand we can thrive knowing only a subset of the total inventory of other types of words. In addition you must consider nouns that have been created from verbs (to describe actions or states rather than doing or experiencing them) known as infinitives (usually to describe something that is intended to happen) and gerunds (usually describing something that has happened before or is ongoing).

Verbs (fixed): Verbs are the most structured and rigid grammatical constructs; therefore, in many ways they are the easiest to learn once the constructs are recognised. These constructs and contexts should be studied by looking at all of the choices and associated contextual meanings. This should focus on the way the verbs are used, not on the meaning of the individual verbs, as these can be looked up in a reference book once the use has been determined.

SUB-TYPE CONSTRUCTS

Sub-types are used to vary the meaning inherent in the main type and sentence structures in order to add nuance or to create a better mental 'picture' in the mind of the listener or reader. They can also be used instead of the main constructs to add further detail to something that is already known (pronouns), to create a purely mental (abstract) image of what is being discussed (adjectives) or to get more information (questions).

Adjectives: These can be regarded as an adjunct to nouns. Nouns are how we understand our world, allowing us to visualise, or at least understand, whatever it is being talked about. In other words they refer to factual objects that we know to exist. Adjectives, on the other hand, tend to be based purely on imagination as we all relate to the things described by adjectives in a different way. A simple example is how a colour blind person imagines 'red' to how everyone else imagines it. Because they are imaginative constructs, adjectives, when used alone, describe abstract or relative concepts (like physical, mental or emotional states) and could almost be considered to be imaginative versions of nouns. They can also be used to clarify or add imaginative concepts to noun phrases and also act as standalone abstract references.

Conjunctions: Conjunctions are used to add words, phrases or complete sentences to the text, primarily in order to add clarity. In grammar they have a number of names associated with them (such as markers, conjunctions, conjunctive adverbs or subordinating conjunctives) but they all work in the same way, to add the 'glue' to bind grammatical structures together.

Pronouns: These are a subset of nouns. They are used in the same way as previously known nouns prefaced with **the**.

Infinitives: Infinitives are mainly used to indicate intent (usually after a verb and before a noun) or what something is used for.

Questions: These can be regarded as a subset of verbs as they generally involve verb/subject manipulation and a fairly rigid structure. The majority of question types involve subject/verb inversion (swapping) with so called 'wh' question words used to specify the type of answer that is expected.

MAKING VARIABLES

There are two constructs that are variable. The first are **adverbs**, which provide more details about the action or state, including the dimensional, characteristic or spatial qualities, that the objects and/or players in the sentence are witnessing, enacting or experiencing and the second are **nouns**, which describe the static objects or players in a sentence.

Adverbs: Adverbs add extra information to whatever action has taken place, is taking place or will take place. They are not required in the sentence but they answer questions about things like dates, methods, magnitudes or places. They can also add extra detail to adjectives and to join sentences of equal weight together. They can be in the form of single words, where they answer questions such as the manner in which something is done (how), the place where it was done (where), when it was done (when), the degree of what was done (how much) or the number of times it was done in a given time period (how often).

In order to provide answers to question that require complex answers they can take the form of prepositional phrases in order to answer questions above plus the cause of something, the content of something or the direction of travel. Prepositional phrases can generally be used to replace single word adverbs in order to add more detail - the prepositions reference in this series give examples for each of the prepositions in the corpus - and follow a particular pattern:

Preposition   Noun

The structure of the noun can vary, but the principle remains the same, where the preposition itself is used to announce that extra information is being given and then the noun provides the information. The noun can take a number of forms depending on the complexity of the information. For example, using the intransitive verb, go, we can use any of the following to add the information:

I went *there* (<u>simple adverb</u>)

I went *to* <u>the big park</u> (***prepositional*** phrase using a <u>noun phrase</u>)

I went *to* <u>that place we know</u> (using a <u>noun clause</u>)

Finally, if you need to associate an action, rather than a static image, to the extra detail you can add an adverb clause.

I went <u>where I always go</u> (<u>adverb clause</u>)

Nouns: Nouns are the heart of a sentence as they are the objects which do things, have things done to them or are used in order to create the result. They depend on the listener or reader having a mental image of what they are or represent and therefore they tend to be surrounded by extra detail, usually in the form of adjectives, in order to provide an exact picture. For example, we all know people and their mental image is recalled using their name. So, we can say something like 'I saw **Kate** today', where Kate is the noun. Which is fine if we only known one Kate, but what if we know more than one? In that case we can add an adjective to clarify what Kate we have in mind, usually by noting a particular attribute, so our sentence could read 'I saw blond **Kate** today', this is known as a noun phrase and can comprise of a number of preceding adjectives such as in the sentence 'I saw tall, beautiful, blond **Kate** today'.

Another way is to add another noun in order to create a compound noun, in which case our sentence could read 'I saw **Kate Jones** today'. If we don't know, or can't remember her name, then we can use a noun clause, so our previous sentence could be, 'I saw **that tall, beautiful blond girl I told you about** today'. Note that in each instance the sentence remains intact, 'I saw...today', with just the noun changing.

If we want to add further attributes to the noun, in the form of an active description, then we can add an adjective clause, so the sentence could now read 'I saw Kate **who I think is very beautiful** today'. Note that the adjective clause is added after the noun and in both instances the adjectives or adjective clauses are adding abstract characteristics to what is a static mental image.

In addition, rather than going through the tedium of describing Kate in every subsequent mention of her in the conversation, we can use a form of shorthand called a **pronoun**. So the sentence and follow on sentence could read 'I saw Kate today. **She** was going to the library'.

Finally, we often want to specify the noun and to do that we precede it with a determiner. In most grammar books determiners are counted as adjectives but in CORE they are treated as separate grammatical structures in order to make them interchangeable.

In CORE, both adverbs and nouns are treated as single entities so they can be interchanged with other constructs of the same type whilst still retaining the correct grammatical structure.

CREATING SENTENCES

Using the constructs created on the previous pages we can now create a sentence. A simple sentence with a subject and object would look something like this:

Determiner	Noun	Verb	Determiner	Noun	(Adverb)
(null)	Fred	is eating	his	lunch	now

The null determiner in the first column is a place marker as we don't use a written determiner with a proper noun. The adverb is in parentheses as it is optional.

Determiner	Noun	Verb	Determiner	Noun	(Adverb)
The	dogs	drank	their	water	(null)

We can leave out elements without affecting the basic structure, for example with intransitive verbs with no objects but with a prepositional phrase to show how they did it (manner).

Determiner	Noun	Verb	Determiner	Noun	(Adverb)
Our	guests	left	(null)	(null)	in a car

We can see that the sentence can be defined in terms of a pattern and in order to help to visualise that pattern we can use colours, either by underlining each construct or by drawing directly onto a transparent overlay. The colours used in CORE are displayed on the back cover of this book and were chosen to provide the most memorable contrasts between the various constructs.

Sentences in CORE are built outwards starting with the chosen word/cluster type, then their associated support words. This is the exact opposite of the 'traditional' gap fill, where the correct type of word is inserted into a pre-written sentence. Although this looks to be harder it gives the benefit that contextually sensitive sentences can be produced, thus making it easier to 'think' the sentence.

The pattern used above is very simple and is a good starting point but more complex sentence structures can be built using more complex patterns and visualised using colours. The colours can be used to visualise the elements in a sub construct in order to see how complex constructs are formed.

PARSING SENTENCES

In order to help to visualise how a sentence is constructed in terms of its grammatical pattern we can go through it word by word using colours to highlight the words. Note, it is always a good idea to look for infinitives first (to + verb) and highlight them first (in orange) so you don't confuse them with prepositional phrases, then look for conjunctions in order to be able to recognise clauses. For example the following sentence:

The students who passed the exam are invited to receive a certificate from the Dean at 1 p.m.

This breaks down into:

The	*determiner*
students	*plural noun*
who	*conjunction*
passed	*verb*
the	*determiner*
exam	*noun*
are invited	*verb*
to receive	*infinitive*
a	*determiner*
certificate	*noun*
from	*preposition*
the	*determiner*
dean	*noun*
at	*preposition*
1	*determiner*
p.m.	*noun*

If we pull out the clause (prefaced with the conjunction) and the prepositional phrases we get:

The students…are invited to receive a certificate (main sentence)

who passed the exam (adjective clause)

from the dean (prepositional phrase)

If we look at the structure of the main sentence we see:

determiner	noun	verb	infinitive	determiner	noun
The	students	are invited	to receive	a	certificate

As we can see this is similar to our original sentence with the addition of an infinitive to express intent. The adjective clause that follows can be regarded as part of the noun as it helps to enhance it. The structure of the clause is similar to that of a sentence where the determiner and noun have been replaced by the pronoun, **who** (referring to the noun [students] that been mentioned earlier).

conjunction	verb	determiner	noun
who	passed	the	exam

This just leaves the prepositional phrases, which, as we discussed earlier, can be regarded as adverbs. The preposition phrases themselves have a fairly rigid structure usually consisting of:

preposition	determiner	optional adjective(s)	noun
from	the	(faculty)	dean
at	1		p.m.

Questions: Questions follow one of two main forms. The first is where the subject and verb the <u>auxiliary verb and subject are swapped</u> (aka inverted). These can be preceded by nothing, a pronoun, or an adjective or adverb form of a determiner. The main forms are:

<u>Are you</u> going?
Open question usually answered with yes or no

Who <u>are you</u> going to the cinema with?
Pronoun question word answered with a noun

Which movie <u>are you</u> going to see?
Dterminer question word answered with a subset of noun choices

Where <u>are you</u> going to see the movie?
Adverb question word answered with a place or time

The other main question form is called a tag question and it usually consists of a sentence followed by (tagged on) a negative form of the verb, with the <u>verb and subject swapped</u>:

The students are seeing the dean, <u>aren't they</u>?

LEARNING WITH CORE

All too often English is taught as an academic subject hedged round with pages of rules that have to be memorised before a sentence can even begin to be constructed.

The philosophy behind CORE is to get straight down to writing grammatically correct sentences simply by plugging in pre-determined, constructs into an existing sentence structures. In other words it is learning by doing.

The way it works is to identify word/phrase clusters as being of a certain grammatical type - such as determiners, verbs, nouns or adverbs - and then substitute them for other words/phrases of the same type that express exactly what is wanting to be said. This was illustrated in the previous section.

In order for it to work the learner will need a fully explained corpus (essentially a detailed list) of sufficient grammatical types/words to cover the overwhelming number of variables. In other words a sufficient breadth to cover over 99% of all situations but not too many to be overwhelming and unwieldy to use. The final corpus used in the methodology uses just over 5,000 words. The biggest group are the nouns of almost 2,000 words, followed by over 1,200 verbs. These words were obtained by scraping documents of all types from around the world with a focus on spoken words (unlike most corpora, which are derived from purely written texts), slang words were then filtered out and, if thought to be important or used enough, included in separate sections (mainly in idiomatic speech in the idioms book). Then the words were categorised into their respective word types, if a word appeared in multiple word types, as many do, their frequency of use in that word type was studied to ascertain whether they warranted inclusion in that word type's corpus. If they were sufficiently commonly used in two or more categories comparisons in their use for each category were included, together with sample sentences, to highlight the differences.

After the sections had been created they were further categorised into use categories to make them easy to find and use. Examples of this are adverbs being categorised into manner, frequency etc or adjectives being categorised into descriptive types, such as positive and negative physical descriptors etc.

These were then written into separate books and their uses were described in detail. The resulting books should be regarded as reference or guidance books rather than 'learning' books. If they were to be categorised they'd fall somewhere between dictionaries and explanatory grammar books. Unlike grammar books they provide copious examples of the word/phrase use in different contexts and some contain exercises to practise self creation based on the principles using the learner's own writing. This allows the learner to create sentences within their own contexts rather than being constrained by those in the grammar book, which they may not understand and would find hard to use in their own work.

In order to parse the word/phrases out of existing sentences the use of colour is recommended. The books themselves are not coloured in order to keep the cost down but the recommended colours are shown on the back cover of this book: the individual book covers are also coloured to reflect the word types being explained. The colour palette was chosen on the basis that they are commonly available in the form of lost cost felt pens and/or coloured pencils and so the methodology can applied at very little cost. The individual colour assignments for each word type were chosen by a focus group who concentrated on the most recognisable resultant patterns once the individual words/phrases had been coloured. This allows the learner to see the grammatical structure of the sentence, particularly common problem types such as prepositions and determiners/articles. Using this method tracing paper can be used to 'lift the word types' from existing sentences by placing it over sentences and then colouring in the words. The resultant pattern can be used to create new grammatically correct sentences without being encumbered by the previous words in the sentence. In this way learners will see that certain sentence structures can be used to express particular grammatical forms (such as statements, questions, travel etc.)

Whilst researching the methodology inherent in CORE particular attention was paid to specific areas of difficulty that students were having in learning how to use English. These specific areas were then studied and simplified by restructuring them. One example of this is how verb tenses are approached; where, instead of saying that continuous/progressive tense consists of a verb plus auxiliary verb it would, instead, consist of a state verb and an adjective.

So 'I am running' is now **I** (pronoun) **am** (state verb stating what follows describes my physical state) **running** (the adjective that describes my physical state). This method simplifies the tense structure as the learner only needs to remember the tense structure of the state verb (a challenge in itself given the various forms of 'be') and then simply append a suitable adjective - with the choice based on the context so the same structure would apply to I am **running**, I am **hot** and I am **tired**, using a present participle, a simple state adjective or a past participle respectively - subsequently guiding the students to use adjectives based on present participles of verbs to talk about ongoing states is far easier than trying to parse tenses. Incidentally, tenses are covered in both the 'conventional' way and using the CORE methodology in the verb books so as not to confuse people who have already grasped the current principles and who merely want to see the nuances of how particular verb tenses are used and what they are used for.

Similarly with determiners, they now contain determiner phrases as well as individual words and they also include words that would 'normally' be regarded as, say, pronouns as determiners. Ask yourself this: if you were a learner you are told a pronoun is used <u>instead</u> of a noun and then you are told to put a 'possessive' pronoun in front of another noun would you be confused? It is far less confusing to regard the possessive pronoun as a determiner - which can be substituted by another determiner if required - than to run though a sort of mental boolean truth table of if A precedes X then it is B. The structure remains the same it is just the nomenclature that is changing.

Another area of difference between current English grammatical text books is in pronunciation. Pronunciation is the key to confidence and it is an important component in the books. It is based on the International Phonetic Alphabet (IPA) and uses the phonemes inherent in 'received' English (previously known as BBC English). This is not because of some sort of cultural imperialism but simply because if the students learn to pronounce all of the received English phonemes correctly then they are more easily understood. Moreover, there are 44 phonemes in received English, which allow more precise enunciation than the 38 in US English (when the early Americans left England they forgot to take most of the diphthongs with them).

Some changes were made in further simplifying the pronunciation of certain words, particularly verb participles, to make them easier to say and understand and an alternate alphabet is proposed. The dedicated pronunciation book covers this important topic in detail; moreover, each book in the CORE reference series features pronunciation for each word/phrase and a common pronunciation exercise. This exercise was carefully designed to include as many of the mouth shape (consonants), tongue position (vowels) and tongue transition (diphthongs) conjunctions as possible so as to provide a good introduction to the spoken language for beginners. It can also be used as a public speaking warm up exercise. Every book contains a short story, in the form of a fairy story, to whimsically introduce learners to the various words types.

Regarding the reference books themselves, each one focuses on the use of a particular word type and covers it in great detail, including copious examples of the word/phrase being used in different circumstances. They also cover such things as the origins of words, differences in pronunciation and spelling between UK and US pronunciation, comparisons of the same word when used in other forms and specific details applicable to that word type (such as collocations used to create phrasal verbs in the verb tables and whether nouns are countable, uncountable or both and whether they are used as verbs). Each word type book has a 'word/phrase/type finder' in place of a conventional index (the table of contents for each book is very comprehensive) so the learner/user can quickly find the right word/phrase/construct to suit their exact requirements. Finally, they also contain information and graphics to assist teachers in the classroom as well as being useful as reference books for individual learners who need to use the language.

In addition there are three books that underpin the reference books and contain an overall view of the language (Glossary), areas where learners make mistakes and a writing book that puts all of the methodology together in a simplified form. Finally, there is a website dedicated to the methodology, which contains discussion, exercises and answers, plus a range of useful tools. It can be found at:

www.coreenglish.club

CORE BOOK SERIES

Introduction

The CORE reference books currently include:

Writing in English: This book provides a step by step approach to how the various words and word clusters covered in the rest of the reference books are used in practise. It ranges from the formation of simple sentences, incrementally adding phrases and clauses in order to create compound and complex sentence structures. It also provides guidance about paragraph writing and leads on to essay and speech writing and structures. At the end of the book there is the CORE basic corpus, arranged by word type, in order for the learner to be able to recognise and change the words in the samples in order to create their own grammar constructs and a master contents for all of the books. It can also be used as pocket guide to writing with or without the rest of the CORE reference materials and would provide a handy guide to learners involved in formal English classes.

Adjectives: This book covers all aspects of adjective use such as placement, creation of comparatives and superlatives, noun substitution and clauses. It also categorizes common adjectives into useful categories in order for the user to choose the ideal adjective to suit their required meaning. There are also an adjective table, featuring all of the recommended adjectives in alphabetical order, together with sample sentences. These sentences have spaces underneath to allow the various word types to be colour coded according to CORE recommendations and/or add user sentences. There are no definitions under the adjectives in the main text are they are regarded as subjective (imaginary), but they are featured in the adjective selector.

Adverbs: This book covers adverbs in depth including such things as: adverb types, adverb placement, comparisons, and clauses. It also lists all of the recommended adverbs together with their meaning, their types, what prepositional phrase could be used to replace them and examples of their use. There is also a comprehensive adverb selector.

Common Mistakes and Pitfalls: This book covers commonly mistaken words and phrases and covers homophones, homonyms, commonly mistaken word comparisons, misspelled words and misused words. Contractions and abbreviations are also commonly misused and so they too appear in this book.

Articles and Determiners: Determiners and their subset, articles, are commonly misused and misunderstood. In fairness, for non-native speakers they are very difficult to use, with the, in particular, being commonly misused or omitted. This book looks at over 400 common noun types and subjects and studies the 'rules' on how **the** is used and the exceptions to these 'rules'. It also covers other types of determiners, including determiner phrases, that are usually referred to as pronouns or adjectives. There is also a determiner selector. It is a reference book for every non native English writer.

Changing (And Making) Words: This book is mainly about where certain types of words come from and how to convert words to other types of words using prefixes and suffixes, plus a section on the roots of many English words derived from languages like Greek and Latin. It also covers French, Latin, Scandinavian, Anglo Saxon, Greek and other source words and phrases that are commonly found in English today together with both their current meanings and their original meanings. It is ideal for creating new brand or product names.

Idioms: The use of English language idioms is a sign of a good understanding of the language; moreover, they are very commonly used and so a comprehensive reference is required to 'translate' them. This book contains over 4,000 of the most commonly used idioms together with their meanings and sample sentences illustrating their use in different contexts.

Key Verbs: This book covers the most commonly used verbs, which are found in over 80% of every day conversations and writing, and should be the first ones learned and thoroughly understood. To assist in this each verb is covered in depth listing each of its meanings, together with sample sentences. In addition there are examples of how the verb is used as or with a prepositional phrase, as an infinitive, with and in clauses, as a gerund, as a phrasal verb, in the passive voice, in its subjunctive form, in its adverb form, in its noun form and in its adjective form. Additionally, its past and present participles and the simple past are covered, with their respective pronunciation, together with whether it is used as a transitive, an intransitive verb or both. Finally its use in every tense for every person, both in the active and, if applicable (e.g. it is transitive), passive voice. The book also contains exercise sheets for every verb so it can be used in a classroom setting or for self study together with the website.

Nouns: This reference book takes a comprehensive look at the use of nouns using a carefully selected corpus that will cover over 99% of general English needs. It covers all of the different types of nouns including countable and uncountable nouns, recognising and creating nouns from other word types, gender specific nouns, compound nouns, portmanteau words, irregular nouns, common collective nouns, noun phrases and noun clauses. In addition it contains sections on nouns grouped by type, for example those use in specific circumstances and a list of recommended nouns together with their pronunciation, whether they are countable, uncountable or both and whether they are concrete, abstract or both. This section contains 1,892 recommended nouns together with sample sentences and definitions, comprised of 973 countable nouns, 239 uncountable nouns, 654 nouns that are both countable and uncountable, 20 nouns that are only ever used in the plural form and 6 that are only ever used in the singular form.

Numbers, Days, Dates and Time: This book takes a comprehensive look at the use of numbers, days, dates and times in English. It covers such topics as how they are presented (numerically or in words), formats, uses and origins. The book also supplies various numerically based tables covering such things as computer numbering, ASCII, including extended ASCII, and other computer based codes as well as tables showing numbers such as UNICODEs and colour codes. There are also various graphics for use in the classroom.

Question forms and other Miscellany: This book takes an in depth look at question formation and their uses in clauses. It also contains a glossary of English terms plus a wealth of other information such as how to recognise and use conditionals, conjunctions, interjections, euphemisms, anagrams, differences between UK and US English, British understatement, oxymorons, palindromes, metaphors and similes. There is also a section listing all the countries of the world together with links to further information.

Phrasal Verbs: phrasal verbs are commonly used in English and usually have a different meaning to the bare infinitive version of the verb. They may also have more than one meaning depending on the context. This book lists 1,500 of the most commonly used phrasal verbs together with over 2,000 meanings and sample sentences. It also has a phrasal verb selector so you can find exactly the right verb.

Prepositions: Prepositions are the most commonly misunderstood words in English, yet they are very commonly used and thus vital to learn. This book takes a comprehensive look at prepositions; covering such topics as what prepositions are, how prepositions can be used as a more comprehensive form of adverb, using prepositions in speech, answering questions using prepositions, categories of prepositions, the origins of common prepositions and the use of prepositions with pronouns, nouns and noun phrases. There is also a preposition selector to help you to find exactly the right preposition to suit your needs. The use of prepositional phrases as adjectives, using prepositions with noun clauses, how prepositions were derived and a list of the most commonly used compound prepositions including meanings and sample sentences are also included. Finally, it takes a comprehensive look at the currently most used prepositions together with their various meanings (they invariably have more than one meaning) and how they are used in various contexts, together with numerous sample sentences.

The alternative to nouns - Pronouns, Infinitives and Gerunds: This book explores the various types of word forms that can be used instead of nouns to change nouns from passive objects to active (verb based) objects and to avoid repetition. The infinitives section covers the formation and use of infinitives to express such things as intent and their use as adjectives and adverbs. It also covers collocations with adjectives and certain verbs and contains a comprehensive list of the most commonly used infinitives, together with sample sentences. There is also a guide to how infinitives and gerunds, based on the same verbs, are used in various contexts.

The gerunds and present participle section highlights the uses of gerunds and how gerunds and present participles, although appearing to be the same, are different. It includes a section containing the 1,000 most commonly used gerunds and present participles showing how they are used in sample sentences. Finally the pronouns section covers the various types of pronouns and there is a pronoun reference section containing all of the commonly used pronouns in use together with a definition of their use, their pronunciation, their type (indefinite, subject, object etc.) and what verb tense needs to be used with them. There are also numerous sample sentences and each pronoun has a comprehensive comment section outlining all aspects of the use of the pronoun in English.

                    Website: www.englishbook.shop

Pronunciation: Correct pronunciation is the key to confidence when learning English and this book focuses on English pronunciation in its many forms. It takes a very comprehensive look at the subject including subjects such as: a short history of English (why we speak like we do), the IPA symbol charts, creating consonant sounds, consonant/letter tables, creating vowel sounds, mouth parts involved in speech, creating diphthong sounds, vowel letter pronunciations, pronouncing the 'ed' ending of verbs and past participles and vowel and diphthong phoneme uses. The uses section covers how individual phonemes are used in various combinations in English words, each of which is accompanied by a large number of sample words, so the learner can practise the sounds of that phoneme within the word structures, and exceptions (and samples) are included to show where and when the pronunciation differs. In addition there is a British English practise section highlighting why British English sounds different to US English. There is also a long vowel and diphthong association section, including US and UK pronunciation differences, a section on stressing words and syllables and also a comprehensive section on the use of silent letters - including the most common words containing silent letters and the history showing why the letters are silent as well as the exceptions. Finally there is a complete set of IPA flashcards, which can be copied and used in the classroom. The pronunciation audio files are available on the website (see below).

Punctuation and Use of Capitals: This book provides a comprehensive guide to the use of both punctuation and capital letters. Each punctuation symbol is covered in depth together with numerous example sentences. Obsolete and rarely used symbols are also covered as well as intellectual property symbols and planetary and astrological symbols. It also covers the use of codes, such as bar codes, QR codes and Morse code. Greek symbols are also covered, both in their upper and lower case forms, together with their various uses in English. There is even a free font that accompanies this book that includes all of the special characters, including things like Braille, Runes and religious symbols (including the Bahai 9 pointed star) amongst others; with a guide on how to easily insert them into your writing. The use of capital letters sections covers such things as using capitals in sentences and in formal correspondence. There is also a section on the use of certain types of punctuation under special circumstances or to add stress.

The Big Verb Book: This book provides comprehensive verb tables that cover all of the CORE recommended verbs. Each table shows the various uses for the verb and contains the past simple, past participle, third person structures and pronunciation. Common collocations are also included giving a guide to their possible use in phrasal verbs. There is also a guide as to what type of verb it is: transitive, intransitive, both intransitive and intransitive, a state verb or a linking verb. There is also a guide to verbs that also function as nouns. Sample sentences are provided in both the active and, if appropriate, the passive voice.

The irregular and regular verbs are covered separately in the book and the irregular verbs generally have comments appended as their use may be subjective (for example some verbs are irregular in UK English and not in US English and vice versa). This book is a pure reference book in that no explanations are provided as these are covered in the verb tenses and questions book. There is a very comprehensive verb finder at the end of the book so the learner can choose exactly the right verb to suit their needs.

Verb Types and Tenses: This book takes an in depth look at the use of verbs in English. It covers such things as action verbs, state verbs, linking verbs, transitive verbs, intransitive verbs, sense verbs, auxiliary verbs, abstract verbs, modal verbs, moods, functions of verb tenses, subject/verb agreement, intransitive verbs, transitive verbs, forming active and passive verb tense constructions, meanings and uses, active voice versus passive voice, which verbs can be made passive and when to use the passive voice.

The verb tense construction pages allow the learner to choose exactly the right tense to use for any given context by providing every use of that tense together with numerous examples, both in the passive and active voice. There is a tense selector at the back of the book which guides you towards the correct verb tense to use and how to use them.

The worksheets that are included with every tense form are designed to be used in the classroom or as personal development within the context of the learner's experience thus making it easier for them to relate the sentences they produce to their everyday life.

THE WORLD OF THOUGHT

A Fairy Story by Kevin Kirk

Welcome to the world of thought. In our world we have an aristocracy, called the pronouns, led by the first person, 'I'. I almost always leads the parade (called sentences in your world) it is present in, unless questions are being asked, in which case I is preceded by its personal bodyguard verb 'am'. 'You' is I's closest confidant and is the second person in the kingdom. Other, less senior, pronouns like he, she and it are the third persons. If I belongs to a group it gets a special status and name, 'we' (the royal we), signifying the group includes the first person.

If I isn't in the group then it is automatically relegated to third position and given the name they. I also has a body double called 'me', as do he (him), she (her), we (us) and they (them) when they are loitering, unprotected, at the end of the parade. 'I' doesn't want 'you' to get above itself so 'you' isn't given a body double and has to share a bodyguard, are, with we and they. The other pronouns have to share a bodyguard, is, with the nouns.

The middle class are called the nouns and their only job is to describe something. The nouns are always trying to achieve a higher status by being recognised by the determiners. The grandest of these is 'the', who, together with its lesser acolytes, 'a' and 'an', have the name 'the articles'. It is considered a great honour for 'the' to walk in front of a noun in the parade marking them out as being special. If 'the' doesn't consider the noun to be worthy (for example 'the' likes rivers and forests but not lakes or cities) then the nouns can hire the lesser (impoverished) pronouns to walk in front of them in the parade as their determiners or even appear instead of them (but I and You are far too grand to do this), giving the impression that they are well known enough not to appear in person. When 'the' makes 'a' or 'an' stand in front of a noun it announces to the world that the noun isn't special at all but is just one of many (the is a bit of a coward and would never do that to a group of nouns – although 'the' will use 'some' to walk in front of uncountable numbers of positive nouns or 'any' in front of ones 'the' considers to be negative or questionable). 'The', being a civil servant, likes to count things - so it often gets numerical pronouns to walk in front of plurals. 'The' is very jealous of 'I' and has a yearning to lead the parade. In written parades 'the' is more popular but in spoken parades 'I' is the still the most popular.

Having very little to do, nouns are constantly striving to appear less boring, so they hire make-up artists, beauticians, hairdressers and PR executives, called adjectives, to walk in front of them. Adjectives boast that they can flatter any noun ('we can make any girl beautiful' it says on their website). Nouns can also hire adjectives to make their rival nouns look ugly or stupid.

The world has a police force, called the prepositions, who walk in front of the nouns telling the subjects where to go, what to do and when to do it. As in your world, the little ones are the most authoritarian; always ordering the kingdom's subjects to go <u>to</u> a place, <u>by</u> a certain time, <u>on</u> a certain day and be either <u>in</u> or <u>out</u> of a place <u>at</u> a specific time. On the other hand the big, fat desk sergeants, like around and about, are far more easy-going.

Then there are the working class; the verbs. They are simple folk and like to do a job once and then relax but they are often made to do repetitive jobs. They have their children (called the 'ings'), who are continually running round and their old people (the 'eds') who like to reminisce about things they did in the past. The problem, for these simple verbs, is that the ings and eds keep getting kidnapped and put to work by the nouns and adjectives. The nouns even give the children a middle class name, 'gerund', whereas the adjectives prefer the name participles ('It reminds us of flowers. Beautiful, exciting, fragrant, tropical, colourful, sensual flowers,' said an adjective spokesword). The gerunds are made to dress up as nouns and talk about the work their parents do, so the nouns can pretend they are workers too. Adjectives make the ings stand in line with other adjectives and categorize nouns or to rush round, while being guarded by an auxiliary, continually doing things for the pronouns or nouns. Meanwhile, the eds are made to go on chat shows and talk about the feelings that the nouns or pronouns are experiencing or their great achievements.

The simple verbs tried to get help from the other tenses but the perfects, being young professionals with no ings of their own, had no time to talk about it. Time is not important to them; it's results that count. And the perfect continuous, being teenagers (they still have a bit of 'ing' in them, even though they try to look grown up by adding 'ed' to their name), spend all their time complaining about how long they've been forced to do something for. The simples did approach the newspaper reporters, the passives, who wrote tear-jerking editorials then went off for long, expensive lunches. They are called passives because they don't do any work themselves they just report and comment on things that other people do and spread gossip (usually without saying who did it, in order to avoid being sued).

                    Website: www.englishbook.shop

Intransitive verbs cannot become reporters as they aren't considered acquisitive enough to require any objects (reporters must acquire objects to write about) and usually summon a police word to walk after them to protect them if an object tries to follow them around (the other words mock them by calling them 'phrasal verbs' to indicate they have lost their true meaning).

The politicians, called the adverbs, were also approached but they were more interested in pretending they had a hand in whatever work it was that the verb was doing. You can tell who they are because they always appear in the parades wherever they like (they have even been known to walk in front of I) in order to show themselves off. So when a poor verb has done the work the adverb pops up to say how, when, where or how difficult it was to do, thus trying to claim the credit. Many of them were adjectives before becoming politicians and give themselves the title 'ly' (like 'mp' in your world) after their name to show they no longer have to indulge in grubby trade nor do they have to deal with nouns, except to grade them and they only do that through an adjective. Other, older ones, like today and tomorrow, can trace their ancestors right back to the prepositional phrases, so they don't need 'ly' to gain the respect they need to lead, or trail, a parade.

The lawyers, the conjunctions, weren't a lot of help either. All they do is add clauses (to make things clearer they say) and spend most of their time giving long winded explanations of nouns or appearing for nouns or adverbs. Some politicians are still involved in their previous legal practises and make a very good living as conjunctive adverbs bringing two equal parties together, but they are always shielded from other, lesser, words by ';' and ','. All of the simple tenses suffer, even the 'irregulars', so named because they are regarded as hippies as they like to do things differently, who tried to give their 'eds' different names to try and disguise them but with limited success.

As far as the punctuation are concerned, nobody ever listens to them, in fact everyone stops talking when they show up. They are there to clear up after the parade has passed and they are often misused. However, the periods are armed with a sickle when questions are being asked, or a club when strong statements are being made, in order to act as a rear-guard. Commas simply clean up part way through long parades, especially when fussy, non-defining conjunctions are involved, and inverted commas just highlight what people say. Not many people seem to know what the colon family does, although there are whispers that the weird looking cousin, semi colon, (the one with a permanent leer) is a sort of super comma and people generally change the subject when the perpetually shocked colon appears.

The pronouns and favoured nouns have their own special category of armed verbs working for them, called the auxiliaries, who had been recruited many years ago, mainly from Germany, and who protect the pronouns by walking just behind them in a parade or standing in front of them when potentially hostile questions are being asked.

They also have their sages, the modals, who, despite changing the entire mood of a parade, are considered useful because they can predict the future or provide reasons why past events are effecting the present.

There are also palace functionaries, called the state verbs, whose job is to provide a link to the adjectives and nouns (a pronoun is far too grand to have direct contact with a mere tradesman like an adjective or a noun) to let people know how or what the pronoun, or favoured noun, is feeling or what they are thinking.

The paralegals, named linking verbs, can be hired by nouns to directly compare themselves with other nouns or even pronouns in order to flatter themselves. Linking verbs, being professionals, rarely exhibit any emotion and tend to just provide a connection between two or more things.

Anyway, I'd love to tell you more about our world but here comes the parade.

Oh dear, 'the' isn't going to like that; being made into a mere object by honouring a simple, unadorned noun like that.

I am leading the parade.

PRONUNCIATION

Read each sentence aloud slowly, pronouncing each word as carefully and properly as you can. Do not pronounce the numbers at the start of each sentence. The underlined parts of the words are the phonemes that correspond to the IPA symbols in the right hand column.

Vowels and Diphthongs	Symbol
1) Each team's dream keeps them lean and mean	iː
2) They mainly aimed to play the same game	eɪ
3) Fred said the dreaded red bed's ahead	e
4) Pretty women hit lit nymph's lips in Italy	ɪ
5) I dried my right eye by Guy's night light	aɪ
6) Oh no Joe don't throw goats at my beau	əʊ
7) After class a sergeant marked father's parked car	ɑː
8) Awed audience applause bored Claudia	ɔː
9) Pulling wool could be good for a full woman	ʊ
10) Whose gruesome true new ewe oozes wooziness	uː
11) Gert hurt germs burning her wormy shirt	ɜː
12) Demure juries sure cure pure manure	ʊə
13) Joyce's moist boys enjoyed choice oysters	ɔɪ
14) Mere seers near here fear tiered deer	ɪə
15) Town clowns frown at brown cows on couches	aʊ
16) A happy cat sat on a plaited mat in Nat's flat	æ
17) Where prayerful bears stare at a mare's hair	eə
18) Father's aggrieved about Italian national cinema	ə
19) Bud loves running up other muddy ruts	ʌ
20) Lots of hot grog rots soggy pods	ɒ

Pronunciation Practise Continued

Consonants	Symbol
1) **P**eter **P**iper **P**icked a **P**eck of **P**ickled **P**epper	p
2) **B**rian's **b**ig **b**rother **b**reeds **b**ad **b**rown **b**ears	b
3) **T**ed **t**ried **T**ony's **t**ame **t**ricks **t**en **t**imes on **T**uesday	t
4) **D**an's **d**usty **d**ogs **d**esperately **d**rink **d**espite **d**ining	d
5) **Ch**urlish **Ch**urches ea**ch** **ch**urn **ch**eddar **ch**eese	tʃ
6) **J**ulie con**j**ures up lar**ge** **j**amborees **d**uring **J**une	dʒ
7) **K**evin **K**irk's **c**aterwauling **c**reates **c**onstant **c**onfusion	k
8) **G**ood **G**reeks **g**ive big **g**arish **g**liders **g**uiltily	g
9) **F**our **f**oul **f**ellows **fl**ooded **F**eltesham **f**en	f
10) **V**iolet's **v**icarious **v**anity **v**eered **v**i**v**idly **v**ertical	v
11) Be**th** **th**inks **th**ings **th**oroughly **th**rough	θ
12) **Th**e te**th**ered bro**th**er bo**th**ered **th**eir mo**th**er	ð
13) **C**itizen **S**am **s**aw **s**everal **c**eremonial **c**edar**s**	s
14) La**z**y **z**oos free**z**e ha**z**ardous **z**ebras	z
15) **Sh**irley **s**ure **sh**ines at **sh**earing gari**sh** **sh**ip**sh**ape **sh**eep	ʃ
16) A**z**ure trea**s**ures lei**s**urely plea**s**ures	ʒ
17) **M**any **m**en **m**ove **m**omentous **m**ountains	m
18) **N**ine **n**urses **kn**ew **n**ewts **gn**awed **n**uts	n
19) A phala**nx** of si**ng**ers weari**ng** ri**ng**s sa**ng** so**ng**s	ŋ
20) **H**ubert's **h**ut **h**appily **h**osted **H**arry's **h**armonium	h
21) **L**ucy **l**ikes **l**ooking at **l**ovely **l**ilac **l**ace	l
22) **R**estless **R**hinos **r**oam **R**wanda's **r**oomy fo**r**ests	r
23) **W**ally **w**ore **w**ellingtons **w**hen it **w**as **w**armly **w**et	w
24) **Y**es **V**ignette's **y**ellow on**i**on **y**ields **y**ards of **y**ogurt	j
*Note: Rwanda is pronounced /ruˈæn.də/	

WHAT ARE PREPOSITIONS

Prepositions are one of the most misunderstood areas in English grammar. They are mainly used to add extra information to or answer unasked questions about a sentence by referring to things such as a place, a time, a way of doing something, or to show the cause or effect of something. They will always precede a noun structure (single noun, noun phrase or noun clause) and can be regarded as adverbs with more information or nuance.

They can normally be removed from the sentence and the sentence will still be grammatically correct. For example, if we look at the following sentence:

I am going.

This sentence is perfectly correct; it features an intransitive verb, so it doesn't need an object, and it states what the person is doing. However, it doesn't say where the person is going or when; so, to do that we can add two prepositional phrases - prepositions followed by noun phrases made up of an optional article, optional adjectives and a noun, like so:

...to the market   (answers question about where)

...in the afternoon   (answers question about when)

So now the complete sentence reads

I am going to the market in the afternoon.

We can add extra information by adding additional prepositional phrases like (new phrases added are in **bold**);

I am going to the market **in the city centre** in the afternoon **on Sunday**. Notice that the new phrases are adding extra information without changing the original sentence and so they can be removed without making the sentence grammatically incorrect, which is a good test of whether something actually is a prepositional phrase. Not only that, they can keep being added to ensure the listener/reader understands exactly what is being said.

For example we could add a time, using a prepositional phrase, after the word **Sunday** (...**Sunday** at 3pm).

USING PREPOSITIONS AS ADVERBS

Prepositions perform similar function to adverbs but with far more information. They can be used in the same places as adverbs; compare the following:

I will **mainly** vote for my party (<u>Adverb</u> of degree).

I will **in the main** vote for my party (<u>Prepositional phrase </u>of degree).

Note that the prepositional phrase, like the adverb, is between the modal verb (will) and the main verb (vote). The following examples show how prepositional phrases can be used instead of single word adverbs:

The job was done **in a professional way** (Manner).

I do my best work **at home** (Place).

I prefer working **in the morning** (Time).

I have **on a number of occasions** worked all night (Frequency).

I agree **to a certain extent** (Degree).

In addition they can, just like adverbs, be placed in various places in the sentence. For example consider the following:

To a certain extent I agree.

I **to a certain extent** agree.

I agree **to a certain extent**.

This is one of the most powerful aspects of prepositional phrases and one of the most common problem areas for anyone learning English, particularly for those languages that do not feature prepositions or only to a limited degree.

Another area where prepositional phrases can be used advantageously instead of single word adverbs is to avoid confusion. For example in the following sentence the word **obviously** can have two different meanings:

I responded **obviously**.

It could mean and be replaced with '**in an expected way**' or '**of course**'. By using the prepositional phrases above the ambiguity is removed.

In the Adverb book in the CORE reference series, the adverb reference section shows a prepositional phrase that can be used instead of the single word adverb.

USING PREPOSITIONS IN SPEECH

In addition to adding extra information to a sentence, prepositions are used to add a certain amount of subtle meaning to a sentence. For example if you say '**We were <u>on</u> the bed**' it implies that, with the use of the word '**<u>on</u>**', we were just innocently lying there, possibly listening to music or chatting. However, if we say '**We were <u>in</u> the bed**', it implies, with the use of the word '**<u>in</u>**', that we were possibly engaged in sexual intercourse.

Other examples are: **I am <u>in</u> my office**, means that I am inside my office; whereas, **I am <u>at</u> the office**, means that I am somewhere close to my office, but not necessarily in it.

Another example is: **He threw it <u>to</u> me**, means that he gently threw it over to me in a friendly way; whereas, **he threw it <u>at</u> me**, means that he used all his force to throw it in order to hurt me. Similarly if I say '**She talked <u>to</u> me**', it means that she used a friendly tone to give me information; whereas, '**She talked <u>at</u> me**', generally means she spoke in a slightly hostile fashion and she didn't let me speak. On the other hand, if I say '**She talked <u>with</u> me**', it means that it was a friendly two-way discussion.

Another use is to describe the recipient of an action, so the sentence '**The injection was given <u>to</u> me**' shows that I was the recipient, whereas '**The injection was given <u>by</u> me**' shows that I was the one who held the syringe.

One very common use of prepositions is to indicate the direction of travel. For example when using the verb '**come**' then you would generally use the preposition '**from**' to indicate the starting point (I **came from** my house); whereas, the verb '**go**' would be used with the preposition '**to**' in order to indicate the destination (I **went to** the market).

Note that in US English any preposition ending in '**wards**' (e.g. backwards, upwards, downwards), indicating movement in a certain direction, would be written and spoken without the trailing '**s**'. Similarly the words '**amongst**' and '**amidst**' in UK English are written '**amid**' and '**among**' in US English.

ANSWERING QUESTIONS

Prepositional phrases can be used for answering questions, in the same way adverbs can, without creating full sentences. The answer assumes the 'missing' parts of the question, so the listener forms a complete thought in their mind.

Adverbs and prepositional phrases are interchangeable, in that the phrase adds more detail than the bare adverb. For example if the question was:

When did you go to the market?

We can answer that question with the single adverb **'yesterday'**. With the assumption that the full, unspoken, answer would be:

I went to the market yesterday.

However, if we went earlier in the day we could use the prepositional phrase **'at 5pm in the afternoon'**. We can then use it in conjunction with the previous adverb, **'yesterday'** which we are now using as part of a compound noun, together with the noun **'afternoon'**, to add yet more details by saying:

At 5pm yesterday afternoon.

You have now given precise details of when you went.

Similarly, the way something is done, where, how often and by how much questions can be answered using prepositional phrases. For example:

Question: How did you fix the broken handle?
Answer: With glue (how it was done).

Question: Where are my car keys?
Answer: On the table (where).

Question: How many times do you go to the gym?
Answer: About twice a week (how often).

Question: How much will it cost to fix my car?
Answer: Around thirty dollars (how much).

RECOGNISING PREPOSITIONS

Prepositions are thought to be one of the most complex aspects in learning English, yet they are very commonly used and so they are crucial to understanding.

Therefore, it is a good idea to practice recognizing prepositions in written work to see their frequency of use and breadth of meaning. The best way to do that is to get a page of English text and simply highlight the prepositions and their attendant phrases in yellow.

In order to avoid marking infinitives - starting with **to** - as prepositions bear the following in mind:

- Prepositions will always be followed by a determiner (even if it is a null determiner).

- Infinitives will always be followed by a verb or even an adverb (called a split infinitive) followed by a verb.

- Prepositions could be followed by <u>adverbs of degree</u> that will precede a noun phrase but never a verb, for example: He was acquitted **on** <u>very</u> dubious grounds.

The table below contains the most common prepositions:

About	Above	Absent	According to	Across	Afore
After	Against	Alias	Along	Alongside	Amid
Among	Anti	Around	As	Astride	At
Bar	Because of	Before	Behind	Below	Beneath
Beside	Besides	Between	Beyond	But	By
Circa	Close to	Concerning	Considering	Cum	Despite
Down	During	Except	Excepting	Failing (that)	Far from
Following	For	From	Given	Going on	Gone
In	Including	Inside	Into	Like	Mid
Minus	Near	Of	Off	On	Onto
Opposite	Out	Out of	Outside	Outside of	Over
Owing to	Past	Pending	Per	Plus	Pro
Regarding	Round	Save	Since	Than	Through
Throughout	Times	To	Toward(s)	Twixt	Under
Underneath	Unlike	Until	Up	Upon	Up to
Upwards Of	Versus	Via	With	Within	Without

PREPOSITION CATEGORIES

The table below shows the type of phrases prepositions preface and the sort of information they are used to convey.

For place	
Location	Show an exact position or a particular place
Inclusion	Being part of somewhere
Exclusion	**Not** being part of somewhere, be away from or not allowed in
Proximity	The state of being close to a place
For showing direction	
Origin	The beginning of something or where it came from
Path	The way somewhere can be reached
Endpoint	The destination or final position of something
For time	
Absolute	An exact time as measured with a clock
Relative	A time that is based upon its relationship to another time
For comparison	
Equality	To show two or more things are of equal, or equivalent, value
Opposition	To show two or more things are opposite or **not** equal
Price	To show the cost of something or what is needed to acquire it
Rate	To show the relative value based on something else
To show content	
Source	What or where something is derived from or came from
Material	What (raw material) it is made from
Subject	What something is about (subject matter)
To indicate manner	
Character	How someone or something is (state)
Manner	How someone does something or how something works
Nature	How someone or something behaves (action)
To show cause	
Cause	Reason why something happened or is in the current state
Effect	The consequences, or likely consequences, of something
Purpose	What end result will be achieved by its use
Use	Reason for something to exist
To add an idiomatic meaning	
Idioms	They can be used to turn statements into idioms

TIME PREPOSITIONS

To designate a precise time use **at**: I will meet you **at** 9 am.

To designate an imprecise time or date then use the word **around**: I will see you there **around** 9 am or I'll be in Cairo **around** the 18th of May.

To designate a precise day use **on**: I will see you **on** Friday.

To designate a precise date use **on**: The exam takes place **on** the 27th. (note the article **the**)

To designate an imprecise date use **in**: I will be there sometime **in** May.

To designate an imprecise point in time use **in**. I worked there **in** 1998.

Note that the word 'weekend' is used in the same context as a place in English so use **at**. Example: Do you want to meet me **at** the weekend (US: **on** the weekend) or **over** the weekend to describe the entirety previous weekend's actions or events.

Prep.	Used for	Example
at	Definite time	**at** 5 am
on	Day or date	**on** Friday the 17th
in	Part of day, month, season or year	**in** the winter of 1985
for	Period of time	I have been studying **for** 3 years
since	Time from a prior event	I've been living here **since** 1985
during	Period of concurrent time used with a noun that indicates a period or event	I worked **during** the day - **period** He slept **during** the lesson - **event**
before	Activity prior to an event	Wash your hands **before** eating
after	Activity subsequent to an event	I got dressed **after** I had my shower
by	Single action that must be performed before or at a set time (*simple tense)*	I *am* always at work **by** 9 am
until (or till)	Continuous activity that will end at a set time (*continuous tense*)	She *is staying* here **until** Friday
from... until	Defines the start and end of an activity	He works **from** dawn **until** dusk
up to	Defines an endpoint	I worked hard right **up to** 5 pm

PREPOSITIONS OF PLACE

Prep.	Use for	Example of Use
around	Somewhere in the vicinity	He lives **around** here
at	Close to a place but maybe not in it	I was **at** school
from	Come this way from somewhere	I came home **from** work
in	Within a place that is not enclosed	I live **in** England
inside	Within a placed that is enclosed	I was locked **inside** the room
on	Indicates a relative position	The library is **on** the left
outside	Not within an enclosed space	I waited **outside** the room
past	Beyond the place being described	I walked **past** the post office
through	Go between	I walked **through** the doorway
to	Go somewhere away from here	I have to go **to** school
towards	Move in the direction of something	I walked **towards** the door
beneath	Placed at lower position but still in sight	I put my bag **beneath** my chair
underneath	Placed at a lower position but out of sight	My passport was buried **underneath** a pile of papers
under	In the act of placing at a lower position	I saw him putting the letter **under** his newspaper
on	Transport you go up to enter or use	I came here **on** a bus/bicycle
in	Transport you go down to enter or use	I came here **in** a taxi/car
by	Indicating how a place was arrived at	I came here **by** bus
at	Indicating a hostile action	He threw it **at** me – He talked **at** me (I couldn't speak)
to	Indicating a friendly action	He threw it **to** me – He talked **to** me (I could speak)

     Website: www.englishbook.shop

PRONOUNS, NOUNS AND PHRASES

Prepositions together with noun phrases are referred to as prepositional (or adverbial) phrases and are very commonly used to replace adverbs, where more detail is needed.

They contain neither a subject nor a verb, but are, instead, used to add snippets of information such as, who, how (manner, frequency or degree), what, why, where or when something was/is/will be done. In order to recognize them study the following sentence: "I put my umbrella by the door."

First we should eliminate the subject (**I**), the verb (**put**) and the object (**my umbrella**) and what we are left with is the prepositional phrase (**by the door**).

In order to check that it is indeed a prepositional phrase we should first of all check that it starts with a preposition, which is does (**by**), and that it answers a question. In this instance it answers a 'where' question, so it is indeed a prepositional phrase.

They may also be used as an adjective telling **which** or **what kind** and this type of prepositional phrase will come right after the noun or pronoun that it adds detail to. The following table contains a list of common prepositions and their use within **prepositional phrases**. The answer column relates to what question the phrase in the sentence is answering.

Preposition	Example of Use	Answers
about	He should be arriving **about 9 am**	When
above	I could see something **above her head.**	Where
according to	It is noon **according to my watch**	How
across	She sat down **across the desk from me**	Where
after	He arrived home **after me**	When
against	I leaned the ladder **against the wall**	Where
along	I often go jogging **along the footpath**	Where
amidst	He always seemed to stay calm **amidst the chaos** (US: amid)	Where
amongst	People are generally happier **amongst their friends** (US among)	Where
around	I will see you there **around 5 pm**	When

Preposition	Example of use	Answers
at	I will meet you **at the coffee shop** I'll see you **at 8 o clock.**	Where When
because of	I can't go swimming **because of my broken leg**	Why
before	You need to get there **before me**	When
behind	I think that there is a superstar **behind you**	Where
below	The submarine slipped majestically **below the surface**	Where
beneath	My dog sleeps **beneath my desk**	Where
beside	We often meet **beside the water cooler**	Where
between	There was no difference **between them** Be here **between 8 and 9**	How When
beyond	The clouds are forming **beyond the horizon**	Where
but	We all enjoyed the trip **but her**	Who
by	I will be arriving **by air** You must be there **by 9 am.**	How When
concerning	I need to talk to you **concerning your behaviour**	What
down	I last saw the dog **down there**	Where
during	I fell out of bed **during the night**	When
except	I eat salad every day **except Wednesdays**	When
for	This strange noise has been happening **for weeks**	How (long)
from	I have just arrived home **from the airport**	Where
in	When you called I was asleep **in bed**	Where
in spite of	I came first in the race **in spite of my sore ankle** (negative)	How
inside	I waited **inside the shop** until the rain finished I will be there **inside an hour.**	Where/ How (long)
instead of	You should go to there **instead of me**	How
into	We should go **into the concert hall**	Where
like	Why can't you study hard **like Paula?**	How
near	According to the map it is **near the lake**	Where
of	He is the cleverest **of all my students**	How
off	Take the boiling pot **off the stove**	Where

Preposition	Example of Use	Answers
on	When we saw flames we knew it was **on fire**	What
onto	She was frightened to go **onto the airplane**	Where
out	He made a quick exit **out the door**	Where
out of	I could see it was **out of reach**	Where
outside	There was a terrible racket going on **outside my house**	Where
over	He had never flown **over the ocean**	Where
past	He went quickly **past me**	Where
regarding	The boss finally made a decision **regarding her promotion**	What
since	I have been living here **since 2007**	When
through	You'll need to go **through the park**	Where
throughout	It kept flashing **throughout the night**	When
to	I'm tired so I have to go **to bed**	Where
towards	What is that thing coming **towards us?** (US: toward)	Where
under	The Eurozone is struggling **under austerity**	What
underneath	I hid the exam **underneath some papers**	Where
until	I waited up for you **until midnight**	How (long)
up	I just saw her go **up there**	Where
upon	You will need to check in **upon arrival**	When
with	I intend to go there **with Arienne**	Ho
within	I will try and get back **within the hour**	When
without	You'll have to go on **without me**	How

USING PREPOSITIONAL PHRASES AS ADJECTIVES

Prepositional phrases can be used as adjectives, often in a humorous way, in order to draw attention to something like something they say often or to the some feature that only occurred at that time and in that space.

Note, how the phrases generally use hyphens to separate the words:

Examples: There goes the **on-your-bike** man.

My boss gave me a **by-the-way** lecture.

The politician gave an **in-your-face** speech.

Use the **for-your-eyes-only-stamp** on this file

PREPOSITIONS WITH GERUNDS

Gerunds (from the Latin *gerundium* - meaning to be carried out) are nouns that describe an action that has been done, is being done or needs doing. In other words they are used to turn the verb into a noun. They are also used to reduce noun clauses (For example: 'I suggest **that you buy** a cheaper computer', would reduce to 'I suggest **buying** a cheaper computer', using a gerund). As nouns they can be prefaced with prepositions to apply the time, place, duration, frequency or method that is applicable to the action being described.

They can take various forms as shown below:

<u>Form 1:</u> **Prepositions** preceding stand alone <u>gerunds</u>.

This form is often used to give advise:

Put on a crash helmet **before** <u>riding</u> your motorcycle.
I told her to read through her essay **after** <u>writing</u> it.

It is also used to talk about sequential events:

Before <u>watching</u> the television program, I made a pot of tea.
After <u>getting</u> up this morning, I had a shower.

Or to discuss outcomes:

He made a lot of money **by** <u>working</u> hard.
In spite of <u>studying</u> he still failed his exams

<u>Form 2:</u> *Adjective* followed by **Preposition** followed by a <u>Gerund</u>

This form is often used to describe the emotion towards the action being portrayed by the gerund:

He was *angry* **at** <u>losing</u> money on a share deal.
She is *crazy* **about** <u>watching</u> horror movies.
They were *sad* **after** <u>hearing</u> the news.

It can also be used to express the level of ability to do the action expressed by the gerund:

John is *good* **at** <u>fixing</u> computers.
Sheila is *hopeless* **at** <u>driving</u>.
We were *prepared* **for** <u>working</u> together.

<u>Form 3</u>: *Noun* followed by **Preposition and** a <u>gerund</u>, often to discuss a reason or an outcome.

I have this *bicycle* **for** <u>keeping</u> fit.   (Reason)
He made his *money* **from** <u>stealing</u>. (Outcome)

The noun could also be in the form of an infinitive to talk about intended sequential actions - note the use of the state verb:

I like *to sleep* **after** <u>praying.</u>
She wants *to drink* coffee **before** <u>working</u>.

The nouns may even take the form of a gerund; for example, to talk about alternative actions.

Web *surfing* **instead of** <u>learning</u> will not help you to get good grades.
Why did you suggest *walking* **against** <u>riding</u> a bicycle?

<u>Form 4</u>: *Verb* followed by a **preposition** and a <u>gerund</u>.

This form is often used:

To show how the action defined by the gerund is/was/will be achieved. For example, study the following sentence:

He *concentrated* **on** <u>studying</u> for his exam (*Concentrated* shows how he intended to achieve the result, **on** shows what his focus was directed towards and <u>studying</u> was the action he most focused on).

Another use is to state action preferences using phrasal verbs.

For example, study the following sentences - in the first sentence the verb changed from *feel* = be in an emotional state | *feel **like*** = really wanting to do. In the second, the verb has been changed from *put* = cause to be in a place or state | *put **off*** = delay an action).

She *feels **like*** <u>dancing</u>. (*Feels **like*** means something that she really wants to do and <u>dancing</u> is the preferred action).

He *put **off*** <u>seeing</u> the doctor (*Put **off*** shows he delayed doing and <u>seeing</u> is the action he delayed).

USING WITH NOUN CLAUSES

If even more information needs to be given than can be provided with a prepositional phrase – such as when the person or the thing (that is the object of the preposition) is unknown or can't be precisely defined – then a noun phrase can be used as the object of the preposition instead of using a prepositional phrase. For example if you want to refer to someone who you are not sure of the name of, you can use a noun clause. So an example sentence for someone who you know the name of (Julie) would be:

I spoke to **Julie.**

Whereas if you didn't know her name you could use a description in the form of a noun clause:

I spoke to **that girl you told me about.**

Noun clauses can be used in prepositional phrases in exactly the same was as noun phrases, or even simple nouns are. For example all of the following sentences use the preposition **to** and refer to the same girl.

I spoke to **Julie.**   (simple noun)

I spoke to **the blond girl.**   (noun phrase)

I spoke to **that girl you took to the dance.**   (noun clause)

Nouns, in the forms shown above, are often used with prepositions to add 'objects' to intransitive verbs. For example the verb die does not have or need an object but it may need extra information to provide a reason.

He died of **cancer.**   (simple noun)

He died of **the black death.**   (noun phrase)

He died of **that disease they can't cure.**   (noun clause)

Note, the noun clauses are used because the speaker doesn't mention the name, possibly because they don't know it or have forgotten it. Noun clauses can be confusing when used with propositions, so on the next page is a table that shows all of the prepositions being used in conjunction with noun clause markers.

NOUN CLAUSE EXAMPLES

The table below shows **prepositions** in use with *noun clauses.*

Preposition	Example Sentence
about	She is still thinking **about** *who she wants to invite.*
above	It must be kept at this temperature **above** *which it will go exothermal.*
according to	She is having a baby **according to** *whoever it was that told me.*
across	We will go **across** *where the water is shallowest.*
after	The ceremony will be at 10 am **after** *which the reception will start.*
against	The boxer said he'd fight **against** *whoever wanted to challenge him.*
alias	The criminal is called Buster **alias** *whatever he's calling himself this week.*
along	Do you have any idea **along** *which route we will be travelling?*
alongside	Could you see **alongside** *which ship the coastguard cutter was drawing?*
amidst	The noise was dreadful **amidst** *which I was expected to concentrate.*
amongst	There was tons of alluvial mud **amongst** *which flecks of gold glittered.*
anti	I am **anti** *whichever laws are brought in that restrict freedom.*
around	We will leave at 6 p.m. **around** *which time the sun should be setting.*
as	It was as big **as** *that whale we saw last week.*
astride	The city sits **astride** *whatever those two counties are called.*
at	I was wondering **at** *what point I should intervene to stop the fight.*
bar	You are all invited **bar** *whoever was banned for causing trouble.*
because of	This book took a long time to produce *because of the really awful layout software I used.*

Preposition	Example Sentence
before	We must wait for the snow to stop **before** *which it is not safe to travel.*
behind	I left the buggy **behind** *where I parked the car*
below	What is the depth **below** *which it is not safe to dive?*
beneath	Do you remember **beneath** *whose seat you left it?*
beside	They were all photographed **beside** *that famous film star.*
besides	They were all welcome **besides** *that man who always causes trouble.*
between	The final is **between** *whichever two teams win their semi-finals.*
beyond	The trees are **beyond** *that field we had our picnic in.*
but	We all agreed **but** *that man wearing the green sweater*
by	The challenge will be undertaken **by** *whoever feels they can participate.*
circa	He was alive **circa** *that time that the inquisition was in full flow.*
concerning	I need to talk to you **concerning** *that incident that happened last week.*
considering	I am surprised they managed to finish **considering** who took part.
cum	This is my shed **cum** *that place where I go to avoid my wife.*
despite	He didn't revise **despite** *which he still managed to pass his exam.*
down	I want to retire **down** *where the sun is always shining.*
during	I took part in the race **during** *which my wheel fell off.*
except	I loved everything about it **except** *when I had to sing.*
excepting	Everyone took part in the marathon **excepting** *that guy with the limp.*
failing	We could go by train **failing** *that we can take a bus.*
following	You will go on stage **following** *that girl who plays the cello.*
for	The offer is open **for** *whoever can pay the fee.*
from	I was glad to escape **from** *that woman who can't stop talking.*

Preposition	Example Sentence
given	He turned out ok **given** *who his parents are.*
going on	It was late **going on** *that time I should have been in my bed.*
in	I will go **in** *whichever car has a free seat.*
including	They all enjoyed it **including** *that guy who normally hates opera.*
inside	It was huge **inside** *that cathedral we visited.*
into	I was wary of being dragged **into** *whatever scheme he was cooking up.*
like	Sometimes I don't like people **like** *whoever it was that scratched my car.*
minus	The final bill includes everything **minus** *however much your deposit was.*
near	It is **near** *that place we saw the accident last year.*
of	He was not sure **of** *what the consequences were likely to be.*
off	This product is way **off** *what the specification calls for.*
on	Can you tell me **on** *which airline you flew.*
onto	We will get **onto** *whichever bus stops here.*
opposite	You can park **opposite** *that restaurant we ate in last night.*
out	I had just got **out** *when the roof came tumbling down.*
out of	This restaurant is always **out of** *whatever I like to eat.*
outside	Did you see the dog **outside** *that house we are supposed to be visiting.*
over	Do you know **over** *which city we will be flying?*
owing to	The event will not go ahead **owing to** *that storm which ripped the roof off.*
past	It had gone **past** *that time we should have left.*
pending	The decision is waiting **pending** *whoever needs to sign off on it.*
per	We should paint our faces blue **per** *that email we got from our boss.*
plus	I will have the soup **plus** *whatever the dish of the day is*
pro	He is always **pro** *whatever event involves free food and pretty girls.*

Preposition	Example Sentence
regarding	I need to talk to you **regarding** *that thing you did with the egg whisk.*
round	I need to wrap it **round** *whichever tree is the strongest.*
save	We can all drink **save** *whoever is driving us home.*
since	I don't trust him **since** *that time he gambled away the club's funds.*
than	It is a lot cleaner **than** *that place we stayed in last year.*
through	A telescope is a thing **through** *which you can see the stars.*
throughout	It was a dreadful movie **throughout** *which the guy behind snored noisily.*
to	We are always attracted **to** *that which we cannot have.*
towards	You all need to move **towards** *that guy who is holding the clipboard.*
under	They repealed the law **under** *which many atrocities were committed.*
underneath	The papers are all **underneath** *that bag the blond girl left.*
unlike	This boy is nice **unlike** *that guy you used to go out with.*
until	We lived peacefully **until** *that day the soldiers arrived.*
up	The balloon will go **up** *whenever it is filled with hot air.*
upon	I arrived **upon** *that train that is waiting over there.*
up to	You will work **up to** *whenever I decide you can stop.*
upwards of	We earned **upwards of** *whatever we expected.*
versus	The choice was starving **versus** *whatever I could find in my fridge.*
via	We will go **via** *that beautiful valley we saw last year.*
vice	You can take the motorcycle **vice** whichever *car you were thinking of taking.*
vis-à-vis	Have you had any thoughts **vis-à-vis** *that thing we discussed last week?*
with	Are you going out **with** *that guy who has a strange stare?*
within	The refugees chose to live **within** *whichever city would take them.*
without	It is not nice to go **without** *whatever you need to survive.*

PHRASAL VERBS

One common use of prepositions is to create phrasal verbs. These are verbs that are followed by a preposition and/or an adverb and generally mean something different to the original verb.

For example, if we take the verb make (meaning: produce or cause) and then add the preposition 'up' to it, we now have another verb that means to either reconcile an argument (We made up after falling out over politics) or to apply cosmetics (She made up her face before going out). A full list of common phrasal verbs is outside the scope of this book (there is another book that focuses purely on phrasal verbs in the CORE series).

Their most powerful function is to allow intransitive verbs to take an object. For example if we take the intransitive verb 'die'; normally, it wouldn't have an object (i.e. He died). By adding the preposition 'of' we can now add an object, such as the word 'cancer', giving us the cause of death.

The sentence would now be: He **died of** cancer.

Now we can not only add simple objects but even clauses. Take the verb, vomit, for example; normally, we'd use it in simple sentences (I drank too much and I vomited). By adding the preposition 'up' we can now describe exactly what it was that I vomited.

The example would be: I vomited up <u>that pizza I ate last night</u> (note the use of the <u>noun clause</u>).

Below are some more common *intransitive verbs* with examples of how they are changed into phrasal verbs using **prepositions** and the <u>nouns</u> (in the form of phrases) that can now be used as objects.

Appear	to	<u>the people</u>
Die	from	<u>natural causes</u>
Fall	to	<u>the ground</u>
Go	to	<u>the market</u>
Grow	up	<u>the wall</u>
Happen	upon	<u>a nice restaurant</u>
Live	out	<u>my life</u>
Run	for	<u>the bus</u>
Sneeze	out	<u>the pepper</u>
Swim	in	<u>the sea</u>

Another useful function of creating phrasal verbs is that intransitive verbs, which can't normally be used in the passive voice, now can. Note: not all intransitive verbs can be changed, for example 'die' is not used in the passive voice, we use 'kill', instead.

So if we re-arrange some of the previous sentences, we get:

The people	*were appeared* to
His life	*was lived* out
The bus	*was run* for
The pepper	*was sneezed* out
The sea	*was swum* in

In the passive voice we don't normally care who undertook the action as the effect on the subject is of most interest to us. For example, if we take a bus we don't normally care who is driving it but only how it was driven:

The bus was driven <u>quickly</u>.

If we do need to know the people undertaking the action we can use the preposition '**by**' to add this information. For example:

The bus was driven quickly   **by** the bus driver

Some verbs indicate a direction by using active or passive voice. One good example is the verb, give. In the active voice it means that it going away from me; whereas, in the passive voice (with me as the subject) it indicates that it is coming towards me (I **was given** a book).

I gave her a book   (Active)
A book was given   (Passive)

In the active voice we know both the giver (I) and the recipient (her) but in the passive voice we may not know the direction. So we would normally add prepositional phrases if we need to let others know who the giver and who the receivers were.

A book was given (original sentence)
...**by** me   (the giver)
...**to** her   (the recipient)

So, the full passive sentence is now: A book was given **by** me **to** her.

It isn't only single word prepositions that can be used in phrasal verbs. Compound prepositions can also be used. Such as:

He *rose* **up from under** the car.

Where **up from under** is the compound preposition.

HOW THEY WERE DERIVED

Prepositions are some of the most powerful words in English as they allow us to clarify exactly where something is in time or space. Many of them came from adverbs (and most can still be used as adverbs), which, in turn were derived from the amalgamation of other word types like adjectives, nouns and even verbs. This process is still going on in English, in the form of compound prepositions (see the next section). In order to understand how they were derived (and continue to evolve) it is worth while looking at some commonly used prepositions to study their origins. The table below shows the derivation of some commonly used prepositions.

Preposition	Derived from
about	This word was derived from joining together the word fragments 'a' (from the Latin meaning 'away from'), + 'be' (meaning 'is') and 'out' (from the Old English 'ut' - meaning 'outside'). This resolved into the Middle English 'aboute', meaning "on the outside of; around the circumference of, surrounding, in the vicinity of, close to, or near".
above	This word was derived from a contraction of the word 'on' and 'bufan' (meaning "over"). It was therefore used to signify that something was from on high and directly over the speaker's head.
across	This word changed from its original meaning over the course of two centuries. Initially it was derived, in the 12th century, from a contraction of the Anglo-French 'an cros' (meaning, "in the shape of a cross"), this over the next century became a-croiz, (meaning "in a crossed position") before becoming, in the 14th century, "acros" (meaning "from one side to another").
after	This word was derived from the Old English word 'off' (originally "æf" meaning "away from") and the suffix 'ter' (meaning 'further'). Thus the original meaning was "further away from".
against	This was derived from the word agenes (meaning "in opposition to"), which can still be found in some regional English accents. The trailing 'st' is thought to have given it a superlative meaning and changed the word from a verb into a preposition.

Preposition	Derived from
alias	This word was derived from the Latin word 'alias' meaning 'in another way', or 'another time' or 'under different circumstances'
amongst	The original Old English word was 'onmang' (meaning "in a crowd") derived from the word "gemengan" (meaning "to mingle") the prefix "ge-" being dropped as it transitioned from a verb into a preposition.
around	This word originated as the phrase "on round" (meaning "along the circumference") and was originally used to mean "here and there with no fixed direction".
before	Originally derived from the prefix "be-" (meaning "from") and the adverb "forana" (meaning "the front").
behind	Originally derived from the prefix "be-" (meaning "from") and the adverb "hindan" (meaning "the rear")
beneath	This was derived from the prefix "be-" (meaning "from") and "neoðan" (meaning "below").
beside	Originally derived from the prefix "be-" (meaning "from") and the adverb "sidan" (meaning "the side"). In Middle English it was used as an adverb meaning "outside".
besides	Originally the suffixed 's' gave the preposition "beside" an adverbial meaning, but the word changed backed to a preposition with the limited meanings of "in addition to" and "otherwise."
between	Originally derived from the prefix "be-" (meaning "from") and the noun "twain" (meaning "the two").
beyond	Originally derived from the prefix "be-" (meaning "from") and the adverb "geond" (meaning "over there").
despite	This came from the old French expression 'en despit de' meaning 'in contempt of'.
inside	Originally derived from the preposition "in" (meaning "among") and the noun "side" (meaning the "inner part") and originally referred to the interior of the human body, in other words, the part that cannot normally be seen.
outside	This preposition, which only came into use in the early 1800s, comprises of the preposition "out" (meaning "away from") and the noun "side" (meaning the "inner part"). The original use was mainly to state "with the exception of".

Preposition	Derived from
outwith	This is a relatively new preposition outside of Scotland but it is becoming more commonly used. It is generally take to mean beyond or way outside of.
per	Originally from the Latin word 'per' meaning 'through', 'by means of', 'during' or 'on account of'. It gradually changed meaning when it was used in French and now means 'for each' or 'to each'
since	This was originally the phrase "sið" (meaning "after") and "ðan" (meaning "that"). In the 1500s the spelling was modernized and the pronunciation softened as it became a preposition meaning "from the time when".
than	Derived from the old English word þan, meaning "in the case of", it shares the same root as **then** (they were spelt the same until 1700).
through	This word originated from the Old English "þurh" (meaning "to pass") and the Latin "trans" (meaning "beyond"). Interestingly the word "þurh" has the same root as the Dutch derived noun "door".
towards	This preposition was derived from the Old English adjective "toweard" (meaning "coming, facing or approaching") with an adverbial suffix "s". Originally it was derived from "to" (meaning "for the purpose of") and "wearde" (meaning "face in the direction of").
under	Originally a prefix meaning 'inferior to' or 'less than' it changed through old English to mean 'subject to' (as in subordinate to), 'beneath' and 'among'. It finally came to be used as a position lower than something else.
upwards	Derived from the Old English "up" (meaning "towards heaven") and "wearde" (meaning "face in the direction of") with an adverbial suffix "s".
versus	Originally derived from the past participle of the Latin verb 'vertere' (meaning to turn) it was used in Latin as 'versus' meaning to turn towards or against.
via	From the Latin 'via' meaning 'by way of'. It was commonly used to describe a road, path or the course of history
within	This word was derived from the Old English words "wið" and "innan" (meaning "against the inside")
without	This word was derived from the Old English words "wið" and "utan" (meaning "against the outside").

COMPOUND PREPOSITIONS

Compound prepositions are formed by prefixing, and/or suffixing, a preposition to another word type like a noun, an adjective, an adverb, a verb participle or another preposition.

They are generally used to be more specific about exactly where something is, to indicate how it is moving or changing position or, very commonly, in idioms. Note that the reference section also contains some commonly used compound prepositions, such as **"according to"** and **"because of"**. In the table the alternate meanings are in **bold** and example sentences are in parentheses (...).

Preposition	Meaning and Example Sentences
across from	**Facing** (I sat **across from** my opponents during the chess tournament). It is generally used to say that something (or example a barrier) is between the two people who are across from each other.
adjacent to	**Next to** (I bought the land **adjacent to** mine so I could extend my lawn). **Next to something but not necessarily touching** (He parked **adjacent to** me).
ahead of	**Long before** (I booked my tickets **ahead of** time to ensure that I could get them.) **In front of** (I was **ahead of** her in the queue so I got served first).
along with	**Accompanied by** (I went to a restaurant last night **along with** my wife). **Together with** (The jewel merchant came to the shop **along with** a body guard).
alongside of	**In addition to** (**Alongside of** his doctorate he had considerable experience). **In parallel with** (The boat was berthed **alongside of** a much bigger ship).
apart from	**Separate from** (She stood **apart from** the other students in the room). **Considered in isolation** (We have finished the project **apart from** the paperwork).
apud	**Quoting primary followed by secondary source** ("I do and I understand": Aristotle **apud** Piaget)
around about	**Estimated time or date** (I will get there **around about** noon *or* he will arrive in the UK **around about** the 15th of June). **Estimated amount** (It will cost **around about** $500 *or* It will require **around about** 50 square metres of concrete).

Preposition	Meaning and Example Sentences
as a consequence of	**Unintended effect** (He crashed his car **as a consequence of** his excessive speed). **Result was caused by an action** (**As a consequence of** the new tax, local companies started closing).
as a result of	This differs from the preposition above in that it usually used to **describe an action or a positive result of a policy** (**As a result of** the new tax the city had more money to spend on social services).
as against	**In contrast to** (He was by far the best student **as against** the rest of his class). **In competition with** (**As against** all other members of the team she was very fast).
as between	Used for **indistinguishable comparisons** (There was little different between them **as between** two peas in a pod). **Judging or choosing between the two** (**As between** the two dresses I couldn't decide which was prettier).
as compared to	Used to <u>contrast</u> something **with something else** (I like tea **as compared to** my wife who prefers juice).
as compared with	Used **to <u>compare</u> two things** (**As compared with** my other dogs he seldom barks).
as for	Used to **add an additional item or person to a conversation** (The class will probably finish the assignment on time, **as for** Philip I am not so sure).
as of	To **signify that something started at a particular time or point** (**As of** today the orchard next door is out of bounds to all students).
as per	**Consistent with** (**As per** protocol the Ambassador was greeted first). **In accordance with** (We delivered the product **as per** your specifications). **According to** (We drew up the contact **as per** your lawyer's suggestions).
aside from	To **indicate an exception** (**Aside from** Sheila, who is sick, they all want to attend the meeting).
at the point of	To say **someone was about to do something** – [+ <u>gerund</u>] (I was **at the point of** <u>calling</u> you when you arrived). To **indicate that an action was forced** (Governments collect taxes **at the point of** a gun).

Preposition	Meaning and Example Sentences
at the time of	**To indicate a time in the past associated with a certain historical era** (The battle took place **at the time of** the roman empire). **Indicate the same time as a specific event** (The accident happened **at the time of** the new moon).
back to	**Return to a specific point** (I had to go **back to** the start). **Turn around** (It was turned **back to** front). **Return to a specific time** (He wanted to go **back to** the 1970s).
by force of	**Using the power of** (The country was taken **by force of** arms). **Doing something through strength of character** (He achieved a lot **by force of** his personality).
by means of	**Through the use of** (She achieved her position **by means of** her intelligence). **How something was done** (I laid out this book **by means of** a DTP system).
by reason of	**On account of** (He was found not guilty of murder **by reason of** insanity). **Give the reason for** (He was given a lower sentence **by reason of** his cooperation).
by way of	**Via** (The burglar entered the house **by way of** an open window). Define a place on a way to a destination (He got to Leeds **by way of** Birmingham).
care of	**Be held by** (You can send the letter to me **care of** the post office in the local town). Note: this is often abbreviated as c/o when written as part of an address.
counter to	**In opposition to** (**Counter to** his assertions, we can prove the claims).
due to	**Because of** (I was unable to eat lunch **due to** a strike in the canteen). **Something that is out of the control of the speaker** (I couldn't get to work **due to** the 10 metre high snowdrifts).
except for	**With the exception of** (The whole board attended the meeting **except for** John who was ill).
far from	**Being a long way from** (We are not **far from** our destination. This is more commonly used as a negative, using not, to say that somewhere is close (The house is **not far from** the park).

Preposition	Meaning and Example Sentences
for the lack of	**Not having** (**For the lack of** something better to do, he watched television).
for fear of	**Being afraid of** [*+ gerund*] (She decided to keep quiet, **for fear of** saying the wrong thing).
for the purpose of	**In order to – this is usually followed by gerund as it refers to an action** (She attends class **for the purpose of** learning English) – **but it can be used in an idiom** - **for the purpose of** this exercise we shall assume…: meaning that something is hypothetical and is there purely to create a scenario for discussion.
for the sake of	**In the interests of** (They hated each other but stayed married **for the sake of** the children).
for the want of	**Usually used to show that the lack of something small led to the loss of something vital** (**For the want of** a few drops of oil the aircraft was lost).
from above	**From a higher position** (the new rules came **from above** my manager's level). **To refer to an action that has been taken by a deity** [God] (The solution can only be granted **from above**) - note, this is an adverb.
from amidst	**From within a group of uncountable things** (She emerged unscathed **from amidst** the chaos)
from amongst	**From within a group of countable things** (He extracted the letter **from amongst** the pile of documents).
from behind	**This is often used to indicate emerging from an inferior position – usually followed by an infinitive** (He came **from behind** the other cars to win the race) or **from a partially obscured place on the same level** (The driver got out **from behind** the wheel).
from beneath	**From a lower, partially obscured place** (He picked it up **from beneath** the table).
from between	**Out from the middle of two things** (I managed to retrieve it **from between** the wall and the radiator)
from over	**From an uncertain direction** – often used when the direction is vague (The ball came **from over** there somewhere, I think).

Uses

Preposition	Meaning and Example Sentences
from under	**From a lower, hidden position** (She retrieved her shoes **from under** the bed)
heretofore	To **describe a situation that has existed up to this point** – it is often used to describe negative situations (**Heretofore** this time the bill hasn't been paid).
hereunder	**In a subsequent part of** (It is better described **hereunder** the advertisement). This is mainly used as an adverb.
in a place of	**Describing a preferred place** (I want to die **in a place of** my choosing). Note the difference with **in place of**.
in accordance with	**Following the previously agreed terms of** (In **accordance with** your instructions, we are cancelling the order and refunding your money).
in addition to	**Added responsibility or benefit** (In **addition to** your regular salary you will be given a housing allowance).
in agreement with	**Something done according to the rules, laws, opinion or contractual arrangement** (The action must be undertaken **in agreement with** our core principles).
in between	**In the middle of two events or things** (In between cooking and cleaning she had no time to relax [events]. Never get **in between** a mother and her daughter when they are arguing [people/things]).
in the care of	**In the custody of** (We left the cat **in the care of** the next door neighbours).
in case of	**In the event of** (In case of fire do not use the lift but take the stairs instead.)
in charge of	**Having control of** (He was **in charge of** the bus when it crashed). **Be responsible for** (He is **in charge of** the troops under his command).
in close connection with	**In joint operation with** (Our company works **in close connection with** our parent company in the USA). Note the difference with **in connection with.**
in common with	**Having the same nature or behaviour as** (In common with other aircraft of its type it had rotary engines).
in compliance with	**Adhering to** (We had to shut the generator down while we made modifications **in compliance with** the new safety procedures).

Preposition	Meaning and Example Sentences
in connection with	**As a result of** (I had to visit my customer **in connection with** his sales enquiry.) **To refer to** (I need to talk to you **in connection with** the project).
in consideration of	**Taking into account** (**In consideration of** failing to attend class he was suspended from the program). **Reason for a concession** (**In consideration of** your request for leniency I am not sending you to jail).
in place of	**Instead of** (I'll have tea **in place of** coffee, today). **In exchange for** (I took the refund **in place of** a new one).
in regard to	**About** (**In regard to** the problem that was preventing our departure, it has now been fixed).
in search of	**Seeking** (I am **in search of** any books about my old home town.)
in spite of	**Disregarding** (We went ahead with the protest **in spite of** the threats made against us.) **Against opposition to** (He continued speaking **in spite of** the the demonstrators).
in terms of	**From the point of view of** (**In terms of** talent the two players were equally matched.)
in the course of	**During** (**In the course of history** many wars have been caused by misunderstandings.)
in the event of	**When there is something happening** (Do not use the elevator **in the event of** a fire.)
in the face of	**Confronted by** (The General was calm **in the face of** the enemy.) **Challenged by** (He kept sailing **in the face of** the storm).
in the terms of	**Included within an agreement** (It is written **in the terms of** the contract that delivery is C.I.F.)
independently of	**Without reference to** (The team reached a just conclusion **independently of** the official enquiry.)
inside of	**Within a time or place** (He promised to return **inside of** 10 minutes [time] or She has never set foot **inside of** my house [place].)
inside from	**From the outside to the inside** (He came **inside from** the cold.)
instead of	**As an alternative to** (He offered to go with her **instead of** sitting at home watching the TV all day.)

Preposition	Meaning and Example Sentences
off of	**Up from** (Get **off of** your bed and give me some help.) **Down from** (Can you reach up and get it **off of** the shelf?)
on account of	Formal version of **because of** (The office was closed **on account of** the staff party.)
on behalf of	**Speaking or acting as a representative of** (**On behalf** of the organisers I'd like to welcome you.)
on the part of	**Coming from** (I welcomed the enthusiasm **on the part of** the people taking part.)
on the point of	**Just about to** [+*gerund*] (I was **on the point of** *going* home when my boss came in). **Being forced by** (He was robbed **on the point of** a knife.)
on the tip of	**Close to but not quite on** (His name is **on the tip of** my tongue. - Meaning: I can't quite remember)
on top of	**In place on the highest surface of** (He was sitting **on top of** my car.). **In addition to** (**On top of** everything else it started to rain.)
opposite to	**Indicate a contrary thing** (The product they sent was **opposite to** what I actually wanted).
other than	**Provide an exclusion** (**Other than** my headache I feel fine).
out from	**Emerge from a concealed place** (He emerged **out from** where he was hiding and startled her).
out from under	**Away from difficulty or danger** (I got **out from under** the investment scheme before it collapsed.)
outwith	**Outside** (He parked his car **outwith** his drive). **Beyond** (It is **outwith** those trees). Note: It is a single word unlike **out with**. - See below.
out with	**Make known immediately** (Come on, **out with** it if you know what happened.) Mainly idiomatic.
outside of	**Beyond the limits of** (He lived **outside of** town on a farm - No-one **outside of** this room must know.)
owing to	**Because of** (**Owing to** restrictions on the number of free places we had to stop accepting bookings.)
previous to	**Before a certain time** (**Previous to** the conversion it was a plastics factory.)

Preposition	Meaning and Example Sentences
prior to	**Just before (Prior to** his appointment he waited outside.)
pursuant to	**In accordance with** (You are being arrested **pursuant to** the misuse of drugs act). Formal use
regardless of	**Irrespective of** (We accept all applicants **regardless of** financial status.)
related to	**In connection with** (He had a lot of prestige **related to** his job.) Connected to a thing - **relating to** is for a person.
relating to	**To connect to or associate with** (He had a lot of trouble **relating to** his wife after she had the baby.)
relative to	**In comparison to** (My new phone is much quicker **relative to** my last one.) Mainly formal use.
round about	**Approximate concurrent time** (She is expected to arrive **round about** the same time as her sister.)
short of	**With the ultimate exception of (Short of** moving house I don't know how I can get respite from my noisy neighbours.)
under the cover of	**Concealed by** (The soldiers crept up on the enemy **under the cover of** darkness.)
up against	**Having to cope with** (I was **up against** a tight deadline to finish the project.)
up from under	**Rise from a hidden place** (He came **up from under** the sea and climbed into the boat).
up until	**As far as a set time/date** (I will work **up until** 6 p.m. - We can work on it **up until** the deadline on the 7th.)
what with	**With consideration of (What with** the car not starting and missing the bus I am not having a good day.)
with a view to	**With the intention of** (I started saving **with a view to** buying a new car.)
with reference to	Formal version of **about (With reference to** your letter I can confirm we are currently studying the problem.)
with regards to	Formal version of **concerning (With regards to** your request for a price we are sending you a quotation).
with the intention of	**Towards the end goal of** (He studied hard **with the intention of** getting a good job.)
without regard to	**With no concern for** (He dashed into the burning building **without regard to** his personal safety.)

PRONUNCIATIONS

About	əˈbaʊt	Above	əˈbʌv	Absent	ˈæb.sənt
According to	əˈkɔːdɪŋ tuː	Across	əˈkrɒs	Afore	əˈfɔːr
After	ˈɑːf.tər	Against	əˈgentst	Alias	ˈeɪ.li.əs
Along	əˈlɒŋ	Alongside	əˌlɒŋˈsaɪd	Amidst	əˈmɪdst
Amongst	əˈmʌŋst	Anti	ˈæn.ti	Apropos	ˌæp.rəˈpəʊ
As	æz	Around	əˈraʊnd	Assuming	əˈsjuːmɪŋ
Astride	əˈstraɪd	At	æt	Bar	bɑːr
Because of	bɪˈkəz əv	Behind	bɪˈhaɪnd	Before	bɪˈfɔːr
Below	bɪˈləʊ	Beneath	bɪˈniːθ	But	bʌt
Beside	bɪˈsaɪd	Besides	bɪˈsaɪdz	Between	bɪˈtwiːn
Beyond	biˈjɒnd	By	baɪ	Circa	ˈsɜː.kə
Close to	kləʊz tuː	Come	kʌm	Concerning	kənˈsɜː.nɪ
Considering	kənˈsɪd.ər.ɪŋ	Cum	kʌm	Despite	dɪˈspaɪt
Down	daʊn	During	ˈdjʊə.rɪŋ	Excluding	ɪkˈskluː.dɪŋ
Except	ɪkˈsept	Excepting	ɪkˈseptɪŋ	Failing	ˈfeɪ.lɪŋ
Far from	fɑːr frɒm	For	fɔːr	From	frɒm
Following	ˈfɒl.əʊ.ɪŋ	Given	ˈgɪv.ən	Going on	ˈgəʊ.ɪŋ ɒn
Gone	gɒn	In	ɪn	Inside	ɪnˈsaɪd
Into	ˈɪn.tuː	Lacking	ˈlæk.ɪŋ	Less	les
Like	laɪk	Mid	mɪd	Minus	ˈmaɪ.nəs
Near	nɪər	Near to	nɪər tuː	Next to	neks tuː
Of	ɒv	Off	ɒf	On	ɒn
Notwithstanding	ˌnɒt.wɪðˈstæn.dɪŋ	Onto	ˈɒn.tu	Opposite	ˈɒp.ə.zɪ
Out	aʊt	Out of	aʊt ɒv	Outside	aʊtˈsaɪd
Outside of	ˌaʊtˈsaɪd ɒv	Over	ˈəʊ.və	Owing to	ˈəʊ.ɪŋ tuː
Pace	peɪs	Past	pɑːst	Pending	ˈpen.dɪŋ
Per	pɜːr	Plus	plʌs	Post	pəʊst
Preceding	prɪˈsiː.dɪŋ	Pro	prəʊ	Qua	kwɑː
Re	riː	Regarding	rɪˈgɑː.dɪŋ	Round	raʊnd
Sans	sænz	Save	seɪv	Short	ʃɔːt
Since	sɪnts	Than	ðæn	Through	θruː
Throughout	θruːˈaʊt	Till	tɪl	Times	taɪmz
To	tuː	Toward(s)	təˈwɔːdz	Twixt	twɪkst
Under	ˈʌn.dər	Underneath	ˌʌn.dəˈniːθ	Unlike	ʌnˈlaɪk
Until	ənˈtɪl	Unto	ˈʌn.tuː	Up to	ʌp tuː
Up	ʌp	Upon	əˈpɒn	Upwards of	ˈʌp.wədz ɒv
Uptill	ʌptɪl	Versus	ˈvɜː.səs	Via	vaɪə
Vice	vaɪs	Vis-à-vis	ˌvɪz.əˈviː	With	wɪð
Within	wɪˈðɪn	Without	wɪˈðaʊt		

REFERENCE SECTION

The following pages list all of the commonly used prepositions in depth. The format is:

Definition: The main definition(s) occurs after the title word/phrase.

Uses: This section describes the uses to which the preposition is put.

Replacement: This provides an alternative word/cluster that can be used instead of the headline preposition.

Other versions: If the preposition also has different uses, as in different word types, these will be listed as to the type (for example, noun, adjective, verb etc.), together with examples of their use.

Categories: these sentences show how the preposition on each page is used in the various categories, using two example sentences for each category. The categories can be found at the start of this book (under uses of prepositions).

Note: if the uses and/or the categories are larger than can fit on one page the preposition's entry will be spread over two facing pages. Therefore, the prepositions are not in strict alphabetical order.

ABOUT

Concerning *or* relating to something else

This preposition is used:

To indicate that the exact value is not known (it is **about** 10 o'clock *or* it should cost **about** ten dollars)

For giving a reason (I need to find out **about** the requirements *or* I knew nothing **about** the accident)

For making a guess (I live **about** ten kilometres from the city *or* I will get there **about** 5 p.m.).

For showing that something is imminent or overdue (The game is starting **about** now *or* It is **about** time we started the meeting).

It can also be used as an idiom to indicate that someone, usually the speaker or the group the speaker is part of, has been kept waiting (It is **about** time you showed up)

Categories

Cause/Reason

I would like to talk to you **about** your grades.
What do you know **about** calculus?

Time

I can meet you **about** 5 p.m.
The race is starting **about** now.

Place

It is **about** two miles away.
If I were to guess, I'd say it's **about** 7 feet away.

Idiomatic use

Everything is not **about** you. (Stop trying to draw attention to yourself)
It is **about** that time (we need to do something now)

                    Website: www.englishbook.shop

ABOVE

Indicating a higher position than something else

This preposition is used to indicate that something is at a higher place and is not touching – if it is touching use **on** instead. For example an aircraft would be above you as it is not touching you. The difference between **above** and **over** is that **over** usually implies movement, whereas above can indicate either non-movement or movement.

It is used to indicate:

Being at a higher position in a list or table (her name appears **above** mine in the telephone directory).

Being ahead of others (She is **above** the rest of the contestants in the leadership contest).

Being on top of (He wore a coat **above** his other clothes).

Being further north than (Scotland is **above** England).

Leading (Manchester United is **above** Chelsea in the league)

Being too proud to do something low (He is **above** petty office politics)

Have a preference for (She loves her son **above** her daughters)

Having surpassed (The takings were **above** what we took last year)

Replacement (**over**).

Categories

Place

It's on the shelf directly **above** your head.
Her name was **above** his in the cast list.

Manner

I thought you were **above** spreading that sort of petty gossip.
She is not **above** claiming special privileges due to her status.

Idiomatic use

That decision is **above** my pay-grade (US: it is beyond my power)
He is **above** suspicion. (He has an excellent moral character)

ABSENT

Not present *or* without *or* no more

This word is most commonly used as an adjective (Let us drink to our **absent** friends *or* He was **absent** from the class today). When used as a preposition it tends to be used in formal settings. It is also commonly used in legal texts to signify that something is missing.

It was derived from the Latin verb, absens meaning to be away from.

It is used for:

Referring to a lack of things like objections to a course of action (**Absent** any further questions I am declaring this meeting closed).

Refer to something or someone that isn't there; especially if the thing or person is expected to be there (We will have to continue the board meeting **absent** the finance director).

Without (The judge ruled him not guilty **absent** any proof of guilt).

Totally lacking (He is **absent** any principles).

Replacement (**without**)

It can be used as a verb , meaning to leave (he **absented** himself from the meeting). It can also be used as an adjective, meaning missing (he was **absent** from the meeting), lost in thought (He has an **absent** stare) or preoccupied with something else (He is an **absent** minded professor).

Categories

Cause

He came to class **absent** his pens and paper.
We will consider the plan approved **absent** any further objections.

Notes

ACCORDING TO

Refer to the source of

Use this preposition:

When referring to something that has been stated, like a set of rules or a reference (**According to** this map we are almost there),

Quoting something that someone else has said (I have two days left from my holiday entitlement **according to** the lady from human resources).

Passing on information gained from a source (**According to** my watch it's time to start the class *or* You must do everything **according to** the rules).

To pass on unverified gossip (**According to** Sheila he has a lover).

This word can be used as the present participle of the verb '**accord**', meaning to go together (We are **according** him the benefit of the doubt.)

It can be replaced with **in accordance with** in some circumstances.

Categories

Character/Manner

He likes to live **according to** his strict, moral code
According to the police he is an habitual criminal.

Content

You must do everything **according to** the regulations .
According to the rules you must wear a uniform.

Place

According to the GPS we're in London, so why does that sign say 'Welcome to Leeds'?
According to the map we need to go another 300 yards.

ACROSS

From one side to the other of something like a road or river

Uses for this word include:

To discuss someone's character (He comes **across** as... = he is like)

To confirm a discovery (come **across** = find)

Extent of a place (it stretches **across** = it covers the whole area)

Give directions (go **across** something like a bridge).

When it is used to describe movement or direction it generally means that it crosses at an angle to the general direction that the thing being crossed (like a river or a road) follows.

It is more commonly used in phrasal verbs than as a stand alone preposition

Categories

Cause

I came **across** a really interesting English grammar book the other day. (Note: It is used to form a phrasal verb - **come across**)
Did you come **across** any interesting places in Thailand?

Manner

I wouldn't like to come **across** him on a dark night.
He comes **across** as a bit of a prude.

Direction

You have no need to go **across** the road to the 7/11.
Go **across** the crossroads then turn left at the next junction.

Place

It stretches right **across** the huge park.
The sky stretched, almost infinitely, **across** the desert.

　　　　　　　Website: www.englishbook.shop

AFORE

At an earlier time

This is an old word that is seldom used these days. It is used to say that something had happened at an earlier time or before some other event. It has passed into common usage as a prefix with the same meaning as stating that something has gone before. For example study the word **aforementioned**, which is an adjective meaning mentioned before. Although archaic, this preposition could have been used as the phrase **afore mentioned** (The subject has been **mentioned afore** in its adverb form). Nowadays, the preposition **before** is commonly used instead.

Categories

Time

I will give you the transcript **afore** my speech
I drink warm milk **afore** bed

Place (mainly naval)

He spent five years **afore** the mast (serving in a wooden ship).
It was stowed **afore** the cargo in the hold.

Notes

AFTER

Following in time, place or order

This word is generally used for describing something that:

Follows in absolute time (I generally get home **after** six p.m.).

Follows in relative time (I'll meet you **after** lunch).

Follows in position (turn right **after** the post office).

Follows a result (I got a good job **after** I finished my degree).

It can also be used for noting inherited personal traits (He takes **after** his father).

Replacement: The words **following** or **subsequent to** can be used instead for time references.

Categories

Cause

They joined the Premier League **after** winning the European cup.
He moved up a set **after** getting a good grade in his exam.

Manner

He takes **after** his father; he was clever too.
He's not so clever **after** all.

Time

I usually watch television **after** tea.
The movie starts sometime **after** 9 p.m.

Place

It's the first left just **after** the big tree.
My house is just **after** the police station on Hawthorne Avenue.

Notes

AGAINST

Be in opposition, or close proximity, to something

This word is generally used for:

Describing resistance to changes (I am **against** the new way of doing things)

Describing position – where something is next to and generally touching something else (He is leaning **against** the wall)

Describing opposition (The police were protecting the public **against** the rioters)

Describing opposing teams or individuals in sporting events (Manchester United played **against** Liverpool).

Replacement (**versus** but only to describe opposition).

Categories

Comparison

I'm sorry I don't have time to chat, I am working **against** the clock.
I'd choose the blue one **against** the green one any day.

Cause

Talking to you is like bangning my head **against** the wall.
He lost the match **against** a better player.

Manner

Manchester United are playing **against** Leeds tonight.
A Luddite is someone who is **against** any technological changes.

Place

My bicycle is leaning **against** the building over there.
Line up **against** the wall in a single file.

Notes

ALIAS

Refer to a false or alternate name

This word is generally used to state a false, assumed or alternative name, often when people want to hide their real name. It can be used multiple times in a sentence before every name that the person is known by (The con man is called Joe Smith, **alias** Mark Jones, **alias** Dirk Thrust).

Replacement (**aka - a**lso known **as** - can be used instead).

Categories

Comparison

Bruce Wayne **alias** Batman.
The criminal, Sid Barlow **alias** Fingers, was last seen heading south.

Notes

ALONG

Follow a path to *or* go forward with

A common use of this word is to state an agreement with something, where it generally forms part of the phrasal verb **go along with** (She generally **goes along with** his schemes).

This preposition can be used to:

Indicate a path to be followed (Go **along** the road until you reach the junction).

Indicate an action to be copied (I sang **along** with the rest of the choir).

To urge someone to go with you (**Come along** and I'll take you there).

To get someone to leave somewhere (**Move along**, there is nothing to see here).

With the verbs **go** or **come** in phrasal verbs, it can used in its adverb form, to state that something will happen later (I **will follow along** shortly). It can also be used with the verb **get** to show people compromising in order to avoid conflict (If we try to see other people's points of view we can all **get along** much better).

Replacement (**next to** *or* **by**).

Categories

Manner

He went **along** with the hair brained plan. – phrasal verb: go along
He just ambles **along** ignoring the rest of the world. - phrasal verb

Direction

Walk **along** the river and you can't miss it.
The towpath goes all the way **along** the canal.

Notes

ALONGSIDE

Be beside *or* move together with *or* do together with

This word can be used:

To show one thing is moving up to something stationary (The ship is being brought **alongside** the dock).

To show two things moving together (The police car drew **alongside** the speeding motorist).

To indicate that something else is being done as an additional activity (I teach computers **alongside** my normal grammar classes).

To show something/someone is moving together with someone else or some other thing (My dog walked **alongside** me).

To show someone is present when something is happening (I spoke to the press **alongside** my wife).

To indicate that something that normally moves is now at rest beside something else (I parked my motorcycle **alongside** her bicycle).

Replacement (**next to**).

Categories

Place

You can park **alongside** the trash cans round the back.
The ship was tied up **alongside** the dock.

Direction

The coastguard cutter came **alongside** the pirate ship.
She drove on a track that ran **alongside** the road.

Manner

I had to do it **alongside** my other work.
He worked in a public hospital **alongside** his private work.

AMID/AMIDST

Be in the middle of, or surrounded by, something

This word is used to indicating being in the middle of or surrounded by something.

It is generally used with uncountable nouns or when describing things that cannot be separated easily, whereas the close synonym **among/amongst**, is used with countable nouns or separable objects or people.

It can be used for the following:

When describing being surrounded by things you can see or touch (I was walking **amidst** the wild flowers)

To describe being surrounded by things you cannot see or touch (I couldn't work **amidst** all the noise).

Both amid and amidst have the same meaning and can be used interchangeably. **Amid** tends to be used more in the USA; whereas, **amidst** tends to be used more in the UK.

Amid/amidst is regarded as being more formal than **among/amongst**.

Amid is joined with the noun **ships** to create the adverb **amidships** meaning in the centre of the ship.

Categories

Place

I sat in the cafe **amidst** the other patrons
I'll never find her **amidst** the crowds of bargain hunters

Notes

AMONG/AMONGST

Being part of, or surrounded by, a group of people or things

You can use this word for in the following scenarios:

To describe happenings between people (Is there anyone **amongst** us who disagrees with the plan?)

To describe being in the middle of a group (She was happiest **amongst** members of her family).

It is generally used with countable nouns and is generally regarded as being less formal than **amid/amidst.**

Among tends to be used more in the USA; whereas, **amongst** is used more in the UK.

Use this preposition when using the object pronoun **us** (Lots of people from different countries live **amongst us**).

Replacement (**surrounded by** - in most cases).

Categories

Place

I have lived **among** the Thai people for years now.
There, **amongst** the recycling bins, she found true love.

Manner

The students finally agreed a study plan **amongst** themselves.
There is honour **amongst** thieves. (US: honor among thieves)

Content

She loathes creepy guys **amongst** other things she hates.
He likes woodwork **among** his other hobbies.

     Website: www.englishbook.shop

ANTI

Being against something

This rarely used word is used:

To indicate opposition to something such as a concept (He is **anti** communism)

To show opposition to a proposal (She is **anti** the new ideas).

It can be used with nouns or noun phrases.

It is more commonly used as an adjective, or prefix, where it is either hyphenated (**anti**-capitalist) or forms part of the word (**anti**social).

Replacement(s) (**against** or **in opposition to**).

Categories

Manner

He is **anti** everything on principle.
He is **anti** the free movement of people across borders.

Notes

APROPOS

Related to *or* connected to

This preposition is used:

To be related to what has just been said (I saw the bank manager yesterday - **apropos** my overdraft).

To be connected to something previously discussed (**Apropos** your decision to leave, I think you are doing the right thing).

To provide a reminder (I got that essay you wrote - **apropos** that don't you still owe me another one?).

It can be used with '**of**', usually to make something sound like it has just occurred to you (**Apropos of** that idea, I seem to recall about something similar I read about in the paper).

Note the use of the comma when using this word.

It can be used as an adjective to mean suitable for an occasion (I think a suit and tie is **apropos** for a job interview).

Categories

Content

Apropos your interview, we are pleased to be able to offer you the job. I would appreciate a reply, **apropos** my last letter.

Notes

AS

To describe the role of *or* the function *or* purpose

This preposition is used for:

Indicating the role (I use my hammer **as** a screwdriver)

To indicate a function (I use this book **as** my English language reference).

To provide the status of something (I am using the folded paper **as** a door stop)

To provide the status of someone (he is serving **as** the temporary chairman).

It is more commonly used as an adverb, particularly when using comparisons. When used as an adverb it is used for: showing that something is to the same degree, or represents the same amount, or is of the same extent, or to show similarity or equality, or when giving an example, or when something or someone is thought to be or considered to be the same or close to someone or something else, or when describing how something is done in a certain way.

It can also be used be used as a conjunction (We got the same result **as** we did last time we tried).

It can also function as a determiner (I thought the same **as** you).

Categories

Cause

He works **as** a computer programmer.
My promotion came **as** quite a shock to me.

Manner

He is **as** good **as** gold. (UK idiom meaning well behaved)
You'll be great **as** a father.

Comparison

It's not worth as much **as** my car.
Chromium oxide's hardness is the same **as** a diamond's.

AROUND

In a position *or* a direction *or* surrounding *or* an approximation

---

This word can be used for the following:

When giving directions (If you go **around** the corner and you'll see it).

To provide approximations (it will cost **around** ten pounds).

To show aimless actions (He is mooching **around** the room)

To describe an approximate area (It is **around** 10 square metres)

To give an approximate time (I will meet you **around** 10 o clock)

To show possible dates (the goods should arrive **around** the 10th of next month).

For showing that something is surrounded (there are flowers planted all **around** the house).

It is very similar in use to the preposition **about** and in general you can use either when talking about approximations.

When referring to time, **around** being used more commonly to refer to the time when something will happen; whereas, **about** tends to be used more commonly to talk about the duration of something.

About tends to be used more commonly in UK English; whereas, **around** tends to be used more in US English.

In UK English they can be used together to indicate a very loose approximation (I would say it'll cost **around about** three hundred pounds).

When talking about approximations the word **approximately** can be used instead.

It is often confused with the word **round** which can be used as a verb, noun, preposition, adverb, adjective or preposition; whereas, **around** can only be used as a preposition or adverb.

The categories for this preposition are on the next page.

Categories

Direction

It's just **around** this corner.

Can you come **around** the back of the house?

Comparison

It costs **around** $50 to go on the ferry.

I only have **around** €30 on me.

Manner

The students crowded **around** their teacher.

Stop pacing **around** the room, you're making me nervous.

Place

It used to be all farms **around** this area when I was young.

He planted trees **around** his house to act as a windbreak.

Time

The match starts **around** 7 this evening.

It takes **around** an hour to get there.

Notes

Reference

ASSUMING

To describe a requirement that should be in place

This preposition is used for:

Indicating something that should be there (**Assuming** <u>that Fred comes</u> we'll have enough people for a quorum - <u>noun clause</u>).

To indicate a conclusion based on something being there (**Assuming** peace, trade should increase in Korea).

To take as being true (The company is in trouble **assuming** these figures are accurate).

To take a position (**Assuming** the lotus position she ignored the noise in the room).

It can be replaced with the preposition **given**.

It is more commonly used as the present participle of the verb, assume, meaning to take for granted, accept without proof, suppose, take personal responsibility or pretend.

There is also an adjective version meaning very imposing.

Many dictionaries list it as a conjunction (followed by that).

Categories

Content

Assuming that the weather forecast is correct, it will rain later.
We will eat at 6 p.m. **assuming** your father gets back on time.

Notes

ASTRIDE

With one part of the whole on each side of something

This word is used for:

Describing sitting with one leg on one side and one of the other (he sat **astride** his motorcycle)

Describe standing with legs in two domains (She is standing **astride** the boundary between the two fields).

Describing standing in the way to impede progress (He stood **astride** the path to stop other people walking on it).

Describe existing across a boundary (Istanbul is situated **astride** the Bosporus)

Describe being across something (the boys were balancing **astride** the fence).

As an adverb it is used to describe standing with the legs apart. It can generally be replaced with the word **across**.

Note the similarity between this preposition and the verb **bestride**.

Categories

Cause

You walk like you've been sitting **astride** a motorcycle all day.
My daughter sat proudly **astride** her new pony.

Place

The disputed temple sits **astride** the borders of Thailand and Cambodia.
London is **astride** the river Thames.

Notes

AT

Give an exact position *or* a particular place or time

This is a very commonly used preposition. Note, it is often replaced by the symbol @ in electronic communications; so, info@gmail.com is actually a noun (info) followed by a prepositional phrase (at gmail.com).

It is used:

To describe the precise location (I am standing **at** the cliff edge).

To describe a general location (I am **at** the train station)

To provide an exact time (I will meet you **at** 10 o clock)

To describe the direction (She ran **at** me like an express train).

To provide the exact cost (it is priced **at** 10,000 yen)

To talk about places, events or things. (I will meet you **at** the bandstand **at** the park).

You should use it when precision is required; for example, when planning a business meeting you should use **at** to show the exact time the meeting will start and when everyone is expected to be present (the meeting will start **at** 11 a.m. in the boardroom), when meeting friends casually then you can use **about** or **around** to give the approximate time for the meeting (I will meet you **around** 11 a.m. in the coffee shop).

When describing a location, use **at** to show that you are close to, or within, a known place (I am **at** the university) or use **in** to show that you are inside the place (I am **in** the university).

The main difference being that the location referred to by **at** may not be the place you intend to be, it is used as a reference point so the other person knows where you are, whereas **in** generally refers to the place to intended to be.

For places it can be replaced with the preposition **near**. It can also be used to show that someone is using hostile or arrogant intentions towards someone else. For example: **she talked <u>at</u> me**, means that she wouldn't let me reply; whereas, **she talked <u>to</u> me** or **she talked <u>with</u> me**, mean that we had a two way discussion. Another example is **he threw the ball <u>at</u> me** means that he wanted to hit, and probably, hurt me with it; whereas, **he threw the ball <u>to</u> me** means that he wanted to pass it to me so I could use it.

AT

Categories

Direction

The runaway car was coming straight **at** us.
He threw the ball **at** me.

Comparison

That's 2 kilos **at** $1 per kilo.
I can change my currency **at** a good rate **at** Krung Thai bank.

Manner

He's good **at** playing the guitar.
She is always talking **at** people. (She never lets anyone else speak)

Place

I'll see you **at** the office later.
Are you going to be **at** the match?

Time

I'll see you there **at** 3 p.m.
The plane arrives **at** 4 this evening.

Notes

BAR

To show exceptions or omissions

This rarely used preposition is primarily used to show exceptions to things. It can be substituted with the words **except** or **but.** It is far more commonly used as a noun, where it is used to indicate a relatively long, evenly shaped piece of some solid substance or a place where drinks are served or as a verb, where it is used to show that someone or something is being stopped from entering or joining in.

Categories

Manner

The Beatles were the most successful band ever, **bar** none.

Everyone left; **bar** old Jake, who said he wasn't going anywhere. (Note that in this example the prepositional phrase is being used as a conjunctive adverb).

Notes

BECAUSE OF

As a result of

This two word (compound) preposition is used to show the reason for something happening. It is only used in front of nouns or noun phrases.

The single word **because** is a conjunction and is used in front of clauses where the reasons are given.

For example: I was late **because of** the traffic uses the preposition **because of** to show that the noun phrase (the traffic) was the reason for the person being late; whereas, I was late **because** the traffic was really bad uses the conjunction **because** to precede the independent clause that describes why the person was late.

Note that both sentences have the same meaning. The phrase **as a result of** can be used instead of this preposition.

Categories

Manner

He failed the course **because of** his reading difficulties.
I finished the exam quickly **because of** my successful revision.

Notes

BEHIND

At the back of *or* be responsible for

This word is mainly used to describe either partially or completely hidden positions or reasons.

Behind is used a lot to form phrasal verbs such as:

Be behind (She **is behind** every problem we have in the office)

Put behind (You need to **put** the past **behind** you – i.e. forget the bad things that have happened in the past),

Get behind (We all **got behind** the candidate = supported)

Stay behind (I had to **stay behind** after class)

Wait behind (I had to **wait behind** until everyone had left).

So some of the sample sentences on the facing page are actually phrasal verbs rather than plain prepositions.

In terms of a place it can refer to something that is:

Completely out of sight (I have parked **behind** the building)

Something that could be seen but is not immediately obvious (you can put your bag on the shelf **behind** mine).

When it is used for giving a reason it is used in a negative sense **to state the reason why bad things have happened or keep happening** (foreign criminals were **behind** the plot to defraud the bank). In this sense the phrase **at the back of** can be used instead.

When it is used with the verbs **get** or **fall** it means that the subject is not being able to keep up with something. So, for example, they may not be able to cope with the work on their course (I **fell behind** with my coursework and I had to drop out of my university) or they can't manage to find their rent or loan repayments when they need to be paid (I **got behind** with my car repayments and the bank repossessed it).

                Website: www.englishbook.shop

BEHIND

Categories

Direction

You'll see it **behind** those railings over there.
You can cut in directly **behind** that bus.

Cause

They were beginning to understand the thinking **behind** his decision.
I bet he is **behind** all this trouble.

Manner

He was falling **behind** in his IT classes.
She was **behind** with the rent.

Place

I'm leaving my bag **behind** my desk.
She is standing **behind** me.

Notes

BEFORE

At or during an earlier time *or* in front of

Use this preposition for describing previous events or positioning, in fact just about anywhere where there is a linear sequence, such as:

Describing prior event in relative time (I arrived **before** her).

Describing an event prior to an absolute time (She got there **before** 10 a.m.).

Describing sequential events in travel (Turn left **before** the traffic lights).

It is a conjunction if it precedes a clause (I arrived minutes **before** she did – where **she did** is the clause).

It can usually be replaced with the more formal word **preceding** when referring to something static.

Categories

Direction

You need to get off the bus just **before** it gets to the park.
Park in the car park **before** my house.

Comparison

She always fed her children **before** herself.
You need to check your mirror **before** changing lanes.

Place

I have to appear **before** the selection committee.
He was summoned to appear **before** the Judge.

Time

Can I see you **before** the end of class?
You need to be at the office **before** 9 a.m. every morning.

  Website: www.englishbook.shop

BELOW

In a lower position on a plane *or* at a lower level

This preposition is used to describe something being in a lower position than something else or in a less senior or exalted position. It differs from the preposition **under** in that **below** usually refers to a two dimensional position, such as one picture hanging at a lower position than another one on a wall (I put the picture of my wife on the wall **below** the picture of the King), rather than a three dimensional position, such as something that is at a lower position but not directly below, such as a dog lying on the floor with a table above it (The dog is **under** the table).

It can also be used to talk about a lower absolute or relative level of something. For example absolute values (It is **below** 0 degrees outside) or relative values (The pay on offer is **below** my usual pay).

It can substituted with the phrase **lower down**, it is also common to use **under** instead of **below** when referring to positions or levels.

Categories

Direction

Can you stand **below** me and hold the ladder.
The Captain went **below** the wheelhouse to the chart room.

Cause

I didn't do very well as I feel **below** par. (Note: par = well balanced)
He can't progress as his marks are well **below** average in all subjects.

Place

Chelsea is **below** Manchester United in the league tables.
The fire started **below** the pile of discarded rags.

BENEATH

Under something else

Use this preposition for:

Describing a lower relative position (The ship's engine is **beneath** the deck)

Describing a lower moral status (What he asked her to do was **beneath** her dignity)

Indicating a social position (She feels that the job she was offered was **beneath** her status).

It can also be used to describe moving something to a lower position (I put the letter **beneath** the pile of papers on my desk) or someone to a lower position (The mechanic slid **beneath** my car to check for oil leaks).

It can also be used to describe something that has been covered up (I found it **beneath** a pile of magazines) or **concealed by something else** (My dog had hidden her bone **beneath** the cushions on the sofa).

Categories

Direction

You'll find it **beneath** that pile of books.

If you look **beneath** this pile of dirty clothes, you'll see the floor.

Cause

She didn't take the job as she thought it was **beneath** her.

He avoided hard work as he thought it was **beneath** his position.

Manner

That remark is **beneath** contempt. (Idiom = disgusting or immoral)

Beneath that gruff exterior there is a kind hearted man.

Place

There is a huge cellar **beneath** my house.

My dog likes to sleep **beneath** my chair.

　　　　　Website: www.englishbook.shop

BUT

Except

Use this word to:

Signify being without something (I brought everything **but** my pen)

Highlight being apart from (Everyone left early **but** him)

To give an exception (I can't give you anything **but** my love).

It can usually be replaced by the word **except**.

There are adverb versions of this word: it can be used formally (She is nothing **but** a young girl) or informally (Everyone, **but** everyone, is going to the party).

There is also a conjunction version (He's clever **but** he's arrogant). This conjunction is the most common use of the word.

The preposition **except** may be used instead.

Categories

Manner

That girl is nothing **but** trouble.
He's anything **but** stupid. (This is idiomatic and means he is really clever but he may not always appear that way.)

Content

All **but** one of them left the party early.
It was the last sighting **but** one that I ever had of it.

Comparison

They are all great **but** this one.
Can you supply any others **but** these?

Idiomatic

Nothing **but** nothing will get me to go to that party. (Used to indicate that the speaker is strongly opposed to the idea or the action).

BESIDE

At the side of *or* next to

Use this preposition to:

Describe something that is next to something else (I left my glasses on the table **beside** my bed)

Be at the side of (I parked my motorcycle **beside** the house)

Not be relevant (That is **beside** the point).

It can also be used for **making physical comparisons** (it looks tall **beside** the other buildings) and **adjacent moral positions** (I will stand **beside** her whatever the court says).

It can be replaced with the phrases **next to** or **adjacent to** when describing a relative position.

Categories

Direction

You can miss it, it's just up there **beside** the road.
You can get there by walking **beside** the canal.

Comparison

He looks really small **beside** his brothers.
You can't really compare Harry Potter **beside** Lord of the Rings.

Manner

She was **beside** herself with grief when her puppy died.
She is always there **beside** her husband in all his decisions.

Place

My house is **beside** the park.
I love to sit **beside** the sea.

　　　　Website: www.englishbook.shop

BESIDES

In addition to

This is a completely different word to **beside** (see opposite); it is used in a completely different way and has a totally different meaning. It is often used to preface a pronoun.

This word is used for:

Indicating when something is in addition to (Who, **besides** yourself, has signed up?)

To verify something is in addition to (There are fifteen other couples in the party **besides** the two couples you have already met)

To introduce or enquire about others (Has anyone **besides** the regulars indicated that they want to go?)

To search for or highlight exceptions (Who likes her **besides** you?)

To introduce or enquire about an alternative (Can't you get anyone else to help you **besides** me?).

It can also be used for adding extra options to a sentence or list. The compound preposition **in addition to** can usually be used instead. It is more analogous to the adverb **also**.

Categories

Manner

Besides English she teaches knitting.

What else can you play **besides** the guitar?

Content

Besides yourself and your girlfriend, who else was in the car?

What's in your bag **besides** your make-up

BETWEEN

In a position or time that separates two things

This preposition has a number of uses, such as:

Representing a choice (I can't decide **between** the red one and the blue one)

Being combined by effort (**Between** us we will succeed)

Being combined in ownership (We only have $10 **between** us)

Being in transit from one place to the other (The road took us **between** two great cities)

Discussing similar places (There is hardly any difference **between** Oxford or Cambridge in terms of architectural merits).

Sharing a secret (**Between** you and me I think they had to get married)

Combine effort to get things done (We need to lift the cupboard **between** us as I can't manage it on my own)

To do things reciprocally – one after the other (it was a simple conversation **between** friends)

Being in a position that separates two things (I sat **between** my daughter and her new boyfriend)

An interval that separates two periods of time (We had a cup of coffee **between** the first and second halves of the game)

To show something that is attached to two adjacent things (the hammock was hung **between** the trees)

Being intermediate in quantity (I only want to pay **between** $100 and $120)

Being intermediate in degree (We had **between** four and five inches of rain last night).

When it is used to describe being in the centre of two things the phrase **in the middle of** can be used instead.

There is an adverb version of this word, which is used to signify an interval (It consists of two one-hour lessons with a break **between**).

BETWEEN

Categories

Direction

Look at that man over there **between** those two policemen.
Go down the alleyway **between** the two rows of houses.

Comparison

The choice of available movies is **between** action and comedy.
There's not much to choose **between** Manchester United and Chelsea.

Manner

She is currently **between** boyfriends.
Actors spend most of their lives **between** movies.

Place

She liked to walk **between** her two big brothers.
The horizon is **between** the sky and the earth.

Time

The event takes place **between** 6 and 9 p.m. this evening.
The competition is open to anyone **between** the ages of eight and eighty.

Notes

BEYOND

Past a limit

This preposition can be used to signify the following:

To be past some point on land (it is **beyond** those trees)

To be past a point in space (Is Saturn **beyond** Jupiter in the solar system?)

To be just out of sight (According to the charts the land is just **beyond** the horizon - note: you could also say '**over** the horizon' instead).

To be out of reach of (it was just **beyond** my reach).

To be greater than a set amount (It was **beyond** my spending limit).

To be on the far side of (My house is **beyond** the park).

To be further away than (It is **beyond** Coventry on the motorway).

To be later than (the discussion went on **beyond** the end of the class).

To be much greater than (Space is so vast it is **beyond** our understanding).

To have problems comprehending (What they did was **beyond** imagination).

It can also be used for comparisons (I'd go **beyond** that and say it was completely irresponsible).

It can be replaced, in most instances, with the compound preposition **further than** or the simple preposition **over.**

There is also an adverb version of this word with the following meanings:

On the far side of (There is a farmhouse with a field **beyond**)

In addition to (They only supply breakfast and nothing **beyond**)

To be further along in time or space (To infinity and **beyond**).

If you want to signify that something is far outside the limit then use the word **way** before **beyond** (It is **way beyond** what we learned on the course *or* it is **way beyond** my bed time).

BEYOND

Categories

Direction

You need to go **beyond** the city limits to find peace and quiet.

The faculty is **beyond** the administration building.

Comparison

That decision is way **beyond** my responsibility.

Her beauty is **beyond** compare.

Manner

She lives way **beyond** her means.

I think your conduct is extremely offensive and **beyond** the pale.

Content

Why he said that is **beyond** me.

It's true **beyond** a shadow of a doubt.

Time

I can't stay here **beyond** 9 p.m.

The lecture went on way **beyond** the two hours we had anticipated.

Notes

Reference

BY

Show something being done or someone doing it or time limit

This is a very commonly used preposition, with uses such as:

To be near (I parked **by** a lamp post)

Be next to (I saw him standing **by** the wall)

To indicate the latest that something can be done (You must be in class **by** 9 a.m.).

State an end time (We will finish here **by** 9 p.m.).

Show who was performing the action – note: this is very commonly used when using the passive voice (The lecture was given **by** the professor).

To show what method was used for something (He did the calculation **by** using a computer).

To indicate the creator of a work (This book was written **by** Kevin Kirk).

To indicate how something continues to be (By the grace of God we survived).

To indicate the cause of a condition (the grand canyon was formed **by** water eroding the rocks over time).

To indicate why an event happened (he got here quickly **by** taking a shortcut).

To indicate the cause of something (He hopes to learn **by** sleeping through the class).

To indicate the means of achieving something (I paid my student loan **by** having two jobs).

To indicate which rule is being followed to achieve a result (She sorted her books **by** the colour of the covers).

To indicate the amount of some progression (The temperature of the furnace increased **by** one hundred degrees per hour).

To show mathematical progression (2 x 4 means multiply two **by** four to get eight).

BY

Uses continued...

To indicate a divisor (Divide it **by** 9 and you'll have your answer).

To indicate a source (I only found out **by** overhearing a conversation).

To indicate an authority (he was sent to prison **by** the judge).

To separate dimensions when describing the size of something (the room measured 20 feet **by** ten feet).

Categories

Direction

Go down **by** the river and you'll see it.
You can get there **by** the number 82 bus.

Place

My wife is always **by** my side.
The bank is **by** the 7/11.

Cause

He was only able to pass **by** cheating.
More and more aircraft are being flown **by** women pilots.

Content

That's fine **by** me.
They travel everywhere **by** bus.

Time

You must be back **by** 6 p.m.
The exhibition will be closed **by** the 9th of June.

Manner

He wouldn't live **by** anyone's rules.
He is an engineer **by** trade and **by** inclination.

Idiomatic Use

By the way when are you going to give me the money you borrowed?
By his lights he is doing the right thing. (According to his beliefs)

CIRCA

Around a certain time or date

This uncommon preposition is used for approximate dates, primarily in historical terms – mainly because we are not sure of the exact dates. It is often used in the abbreviated for C. (Julius Caesar born C. 100 BC). The preposition **around** can be used instead.

Categories

Time

Alexander the Great was born **circa** 630 AD.
Roman emperor Claudius invaded Britain **circa** 46 AD

Notes

     Website: www.englishbook.shop

CLOSE TO

Not far away from

This preposition is mainly used to provide an approximation that is imprecise but near enough for the purpose (Is it **close to** the original?)

It can also be used to indicate close proximity (Don't stand **close to** the edge of the cliff as you may fall down).

It can also be used to state near proximity (**Close to** he is quite handsome).

It can be prefaced with the word **as** to show that it is **as precise as could be achieved given the prevailing limitations** (The scientists reduced the temperature as **close to** absolute zero as they could).

It can also be used with the word **too** to **indicate that something is closer than is allowed, safe** or **cultural correct** (Don't stand too **close to** strangers as you can make them feel uncomfortable).

The preposition **near** can, in most circumstances, be used instead.

Categories

Place

My faculty is **close to** the canteen
He lives **close to** the park.

Manner

That rendition was **close to** perfection
You need to align it **close to** the centre of the disc.

Notes

COME

Indicate a future event

This preposition is used:

To indicate a future event (**Come** the first snows we can go skiing).

To indicate a future period (**Come** Easter we'll hide some eggs for the kids to find)

To indicate a change in state occurring after the present time (**Come** the election we will change the government).

This word is far more likely to be used as a verb, meaning to move towards (Stay there and I will **come** to you), arrive at (How did you **come** to that conclusion?), to reach a state (the pot slowly **came** to the boil), be a product of (A lot of rice **comes** from Thailand), be available in (These cars **come** in a number of different colours), be a native of (I **come** from Cambridge in England), to reach an extent (did the water **come** up to your chest?), cover a certain distance (Did you **come** far?), happen as a result of (Nothing good will **come** of it), arrive at a total (The bill **comes** to $100 exactly), be received (news **is coming** in of an earthquake in Japan), be from a certain bloodline (she **comes** from a rich family), have a priority (my wife and family **come** first) and achieve an orgasm (She **came** when we were having sex).

It originates from the Old English word 'cuman' meaning to happen.

Categories

Time

Come Christmas, we'll find out which children have been good.
Come sunset, good Muslims will break their Ramadan fast.

Notes

   Website: www.englishbook.shop

CONCERNING

About

This preposition is mainly used to express worry about something or that the following discussion will be about something that, if it not corrected, may cause the listener, reader or the wider public, problems later.

It will occur directly in front of the thing that is causing the worry (I need to talk to you **concerning** your poor attendance).

It differs from the similar preposition **regarding** in that **concerning** shows that the subject is bothering the speaker, or writer, whereas **regarding** is merely stating what the subject of the conversation is.

It can also be used as an adjective meaning worrying (The patient is exhibiting **concerning** symptoms - the situation in Asia is concerning).

The prepositions **about** can be used if the subject is only of mild concern, in fact, it is regarded as a more formal way of saying **about** and should be used instead of about in business or professional letters as it shows that you are taking the subject seriously (I am writing to you **concerning** the points you raised in our meeting).

Avoid mistaking it for the present participle of the verb **concern** - meaning to bother – (Why have you been **concerning** yourself with my business?)

Categories

Cause

Your teacher wants to talk to you **concerning** your poor grades.
I am writing to you **concerning** your overdue account.

Notes

CONSIDERING

To mention a particular fact about something

This preposition is used to bring the listener's or readers' attention towards a fact or reason. The preposition **given** can be used instead. Avoid confusing it with the present participle of the verb **consider** - meaning to think about facts or look at things in a serious way – (I have been **considering** my position at the company).

It is far more likely to be used as the present participle of the verb 'consider' meaning to judge or think deeply about.

Categories

Cause

She did pretty well in her exams **considering** her lack of preparation. I'm surprised we made it **considering** the useless map.

Notes

CUM

To have two functions or things that have changed

This preposition is mainly used:

To join two nouns describing something that has two functions or features (It is a workshop **cum** design centre).

To indicate a change (He made a bus **cum** mobile home).

It is not commonly used and when it is, it is commonly suffixed and prefixed with dashes -cum-.

It is also used in slang as a noun to talk about sperm or as a verb to talk about having an orgasm.

Categories

Content

This is my workshop–**cum**-study. (A dual purpose room)
He graduated summa-**cum**-laude, which I think means exceptional.

Notes

DESPITE

Without being prejudiced, influenced or prevented

Use this word for giving a reason for the opposite, or unexpected, thing happening. For every action, or series of actions, there is a logical outcome so, for example, if you are lazy and don't study for your exams it is expected that you would fail. However, if you don't study and still pass then this word would be used to describe why the outcome - of you passing your exam - was unexpected.

It can be used to state a lack of prejudice (The judge was very fair **despite** the fact that the criminal shouted and swore at her).

It can also be used to indicate that influence didn't matter (The police arrested him **despite** his family offering bribes).

It can also be used to indicate that something went ahead despite people trying to prevent it (The march went ahead **despite** the government's opposition to it).

It can be replaced by the formal preposition **notwithstanding** or the phrase **in spite of**.

There is a noun version of this word meaning contempt (He is held in **despite**), but it is not often used.

There is an abbreviation of the word 'spite' (see the entry **'in spite of'** in the compound determiners section). It originated from the French 'en depit de' meaning contempt of.

Categories

Comparison

The match went ahead **despite** the heavy rain.
Despite repeated promises, the government still hasn't tackled corruption.

Manner

He looked cheerful **despite** his almost constant pain.
She couldn't quit smoking **despite** her best intentions.

DOWN

Move to a lower position

This preposition is used to talk about moving to a lower position. This movement could be to a lower physical position, such as a **floor below the one you are currently on** (he ran **down** the stairs) or **lower on a slope** (the bus rolled **down** the hill). Note, when describing movement **down** is often used to mean away from a central place, like a town centre, (I walked **down** the street); whereas, **up** is used to describe moving towards the centre (I drove **up** the street).

It can also be used to mean **moving from one end of something to the other** (The car drove **down** the street).

There is a verb version of this word meaning to drink or eat quickly (He quickly **downed** a glass of milk after eating the curry).

There is an adverb version, meaning almost completely remove (his house burned **down**)

There is a noun version, which is mainly used to describe soft feathers (The pillow was made of duck **down**).

The most common alternative use is an adjective with meanings such as being depressed (She is feeling **down**) or to describe something that is used to go lower (I stood on the **down** escalator). It is often used in phrasal verbs, with many of the examples below being phrasal verbs - look for the word **down** directly following the verb. Its closest match is **lower**, however it cannot be directly substituted in every case.

Categories

Direction

Turn **down** the temperature a bit please; it's too hot in here.
Go **down** the stairs and you'll see a coffee shop on the 2nd floor.

Place

How far **down** the pile of clothes do I need to go to find my tee shirt?
The crippled ship went straight **down** to the bottom of the ocean.

Comparison

They have gone **down** in the league tables.
That hemline needs taking **down** below the knee.

DURING

At some time between the beginning and the end of an action or other time period

---

This preposition is used for **describing concurrent events that happen together for all of a given time** (My wife was making a phone call **during** the whole drive home) or for **one of them occurring at some point while the other event is happening** (I usually have a break for coffee **during** the morning).

It can be replaced with the phrase **at the same time as**.

During is not used to give precise timing, instead, you should use the prepositions **for** or **between** to give precise times (**for** two hours *or* **between** 1 p.m. and 3 p.m.).

Categories

Time

The burglary occurred sometime **during** the night.
Take care walking in deserted areas **during** the hours of darkness.

Manner

He works all night and sleeps **during** the day.
He is always falling asleep **during** class.

Notes

EXCLUDING

Not including (formal)

This preposition is used for **describing something that is not included** and is normally found **in legal documents or disclaimers.**

It can be replaced with the preposition **excepting** (see page 109) but it has a wider range of subjects.

It is used as the present participle of the verb **exclude** meaning to prevent being included or allowed to enter (We **are excluding** you from the club due to your bad behaviour), to shut out (The trees **are excluding** the light), show a lack of inclusion (I note you **are excluding** your taxi fares from your expenses) and not be allowed to take part (We **are excluding** him from the game on Saturday).

Categories

Time

The offer is available any time **excluding** public holidays
Your hours of work are 9 to 5 **excluding** an hour for lunch

Place

They are considering **excluding** him from the meeting.
You can go anywhere on campus **excluding** the private offices.

Notes

EXCEPT

Not including

This preposition is used to **describe everything but**, in other words it is used to **indicate something that is not included** (The price of the car included everything **except** the sales tax).

It can be used as a conjunction (Everyone was picked for the team **except** the man who was useless).

The compound preposition **with the exception that** is commonly used to introduce a clause forming an exception or qualification to something previously stated (She is like her mother **with the exception that** she is much taller).

It can be replaced with the more formal preposition **excluding**, particularly in business correspondence, or with the word **but**.

Categories

Direction

You can go in any direction **except** this one.
Is there another way **except** down this busy road?

Place

All this land is ours **except** for that section over there.
You can go wherever you like in the park **except** for the kid's playground.

Cause

I couldn't take my flight as I had brought everything **except** my passport.
I answered all the questions **except** question two.

Content

Everyone was picked for the team **except** me.
Any transport is acceptable **except** your car.

Time

The restaurant is open every day **except** Sundays.
We're always open **except** for our lunch hour from 12 to 1 p.m.

EXCEPTING

With the exception of (formal)

This preposition is used to **describe a small number of exclusions** and is regarded as being very formal.

It can be used instead of the preposition 'except', particularly when a more formal tone or meaning is required, such as in legal or business documents.

It can be replaced with the preposition **excluding**, which is regarded as being equally formal.

Categories

Content

All the victims have been formally identified **excepting** one.
Excepting myself I left the room.

Notes

FAILING (THAT)

Alternative if something is not possible

This preposition is mainly used for **offering an alternative if something can't be obtained** (We'll buy a map **failing that** we can use the GPS on our phones) or **can't be used** (I will come on the train **failing that** I can take a bus).

The word **that** indicates a noun clause being used to offer comprehensive alternatives that simple nouns may not cover.

It can also be used to indicate an alternative when the preferred option or an option that used to be available, cannot be used.

Take care not to confuse this with the present participle of the verb **fail**: He is **failing** his exams because he didn't study.

It can be replaced with the preposition **barring**, but it isn't a perfect substitute as **barring** is used to show that something isn't allowed, usually for official reasons or on the orders of other people; whereas, **failing** is just used to say that it isn't available,without giving a reason.

Categories

Comparison

Buy your wife a new handbag **failing** that give her some chocolates.
I can only see you on the 10th **failing** that it'll have to be next month.

Notes

                    Website: www.englishbook.shop

FAR FROM

Not close

This preposition is used to **describe a place that is relatively far away** from the place that is being discussed.

It is commonly prefaced with the word **not** to indicate that something is in fact very close (The school is **not far from** the train station), this usage is actually more common in UK English than its use without the negative **not.**

It can also be used **to show progress** (We are **not far from** an agreement)

It is also commonly used in conversations to enquire about whether a place is close to any known landmarks (Is your house **far from** the beach?).

It can be replaced, when used to show a long distance, with the negative phrase **not close to.**

It also has an adverb form indicating that something is not finished (The police enquiries are **far from** complete).

Categories

Place

She lives **far from** civilisation. (Positive use = far away)
My house is **not far from** the university. (Negative use = close to)

Notes

FOR

Towards the intention, purpose, time, price, distance, meaning or duty

This is a very commonly used preposition, in fact it is one of the ten most commonly used words in English, and it has a number of uses such as:

To describe moving towards some place (He headed straight **for** me).

To direct something at (I think this was meant **for** you)

To state the intended recipient (The sticker says it is **for** your eyes only).

To show support (If you are **for** the motion then please raise your hand).

To show a reason (In return **for** your nasty comments I am not going to help you any more).

To show something happened over a period of time (We seemed to drive **for** hours until we saw some lights).

To act on behalf of (I will stand in **for** him while he is sick).

To indicate why something is being done (I am studying **for** my exams).

To indicate a distance to be travelled (You'll need to keep going straight **for** about a mile before you see it).

To show an end result of something (I am saving up **for** a new computer).

To show where someone is going next (I must run **for** the bus or I'll miss it)

To show a purpose (I asked my boss **for** a pay raise),

Indicate surprise at a capability (He looks good **for** a man of his age)

To explain the subject of an infinitive (All I want is **for** you to succeed).

To announce a cricket score (Pakistan declared at 416 **for** 6).

It also has a conjunction form where it means 'because' (She failed her exam **for** she never studied).

FOR

Categories

Direction

Carry on this road **for** ten miles and you can't miss it.
Is this the right road **for** the mall?

Place

I can see **for** miles.
You can walk **for** hours before you see anyone else.

Cause

He was sentenced to fifteen years in prison **for** aggravated theft.
She couldn't talk **for** laughing.

Content

I regularly donate money **for** disadvantaged children.
I use steel **for** making my machines.

Time

I haven't seen you **for** ages.
I was studying **for** three hours last night.

Manner

This is Roger, he works **for** a bank.
He is known **for** his dry wit.

Comparison

Eggs are $1 each or $10 **for** a dozen.
It costs less than $3 **for** a season ticket.

Idiom

It was tit **for** tat (an equal an opposite reaction or result).
He is cruisin **for** a bruisin (urban slang meaning looking for a fight).

Notes

Reference

FROM

Show where, or when, something starts or originates

This preposition has a large number of uses such as:

To show the source of something (I got this briefcase **from** my wife).

To show the provenance of (I come **from** England)

To show the origin of a journey (I came here directly **from** my home).

To show the starting point of something (This cheese comes **from** France).

To show the initial reference of something (Parts of his essay were copied **from** a journal article).

To show separation (2 **from** 6 equals 4)

To show exclusion (He was stopped **from** attending the party).

To show a possible outcome (Insurance protects me **from** unexpected financial shocks).

Other uses include:

To indicate source material (It is made **from** polyester)

To indicate a level (it is only a few centimetres **from** the top of the tank)

To show results of change (Good things often come **from** big changes)

To show cause (Chickens come **from** eggs)

To consider options (I need to differentiate the good points **from** the bad points)

To remove from possession (The teacher took the phone **from** her).

To highlight a difference (I can't tell one **from** the other).

To show a starting position (We moved the products **from** the top shelf)

To have protection against (I wear boots to protect my feet **from** getting wet).

To indicate prevention (the anti-virus program prevents my computer **from** malware).

It is very commonly paired with the verb **come** to form the phrasal verb **come from** (My cell phone **comes from** Korea).

FROM

Categories

Direction

You had best use the A1 if you are driving **from** London.
I **come** from East Anglia, which is in Eastern England.

Place

I live about a mile **from** here.
It's about 20 miles **from** the nearest town.

Cause

He made his money **from** property investments.
He keeps cool by wearing clothing made **from** cotton.

Content

Is this desk made **from** real wood?
The number of employees rose **from** 10 to 200 in three years.

Time

The restaurant is open **from** 9 in the morning until 11 at night.
We can meet up at any time **from** 10 onwards.

Manner

You can't tell he's **from** Asia by looking at him.
He won't take abuse **from** anyone.

Comparison

I can't tell one wine **from** another.
What is the price when you deduct the discount **from** the total?

Notes

Reference

FOLLOWING

After *or* subsequent to

This preposition is **mainly used to say what happened next** (I had a nap **following** my lunch) or **at a later time but in the same way** (I walked along the beach **following** my dog).

This word also has verb version (Why are you **following** me?)

It also has a noun version (His new band has built up quite a **following**).

And an adjective version (The **following** day was really quiet).

When describing subsequent events it can be replaced with the preposition **after**, if it is a simple noun phrase, or **after that** or **after which** if it is used to preface a noun clause.

Categories

Time

Following the ceremony, dinner will be served.
The weeks **following** the start of the new semester were busy for him.

Direction

I went the same way **following** the blonde girl.
We all set off **following** his directions.

Notes

GIVEN

Knowing about *or* considering something

Use this preposition:

For stating a known fact that opposes or supports a statement or action (**given** our current understanding of the situation, we made the right choice not to proceed).

To give consideration to something when considering a proposal or plan of action (I think we need to proceed carefully **given** the fluctuations in interest rates).

The preposition **considering** can be used instead.

There is also a noun version of this word – meaning a known assumption that is taken as fact (As a vegetarian her refusal to eat meat is a **given**).

There is also an adjective version – meaning naturally favouring and followed by the word **to** (I am not **given to** making snap judgements).

Take care not to confuse this with the past participle of the verb **give** – usually followed by the preposition **up** and used as a phrasal verb (He has **given up** trying to become a doctor).

Categories

Comparison

I wouldn't have bought a house in Spain **given** what I know now.
He is remarkably cheerful **given** his terminal cancer.

Notes

GOING ON

Indicate a time or age *or* a near comparative amount

This preposition is used:

To indicate a time in the near future (It is **going on** 10 o clock)

To indicate an age in the near future (She is **going on** thirteen). Note, the exact time or the date – such as the birthday – is not mentioned meaning that the time or the date of the event is not exact.

Another use to **estimate a quantity of something, such as people** (there must have been **going on** 50 people there) or weight (it must weigh **going on** a couple of tons).

It is also used in an ironic way to **say that someone is acting in a way that is in advance of their natural age** (She is 13 **going on** 30), usually when the mannerism is not normal for their real age.

It is used in speech **when the speaker has been asked for the time but doesn't know exactly** so they give what they think is a close approximation (I think it's **going on** 10).

It can be replaced, in most instances, with the word **around**.

Do not confuse this with the present participle of the verb **go** together with the preposition **on** to form the phrasal verb **going on**, which means either to describe the way someone is travelling (I am **going on** an airline) or to say that someone keeps talking about the same thing over and over again (She is always **going on** about what I said to her when I was angry).

Categories

Time

It was **going on** midnight before they eventually left.
It was **going on** winter before the last of the crops were harvested.

Comparison

There must have been **going on** a hundred people there.
There must have been **going on** half our fuel lost through the hole in the side of the tank.

GONE

Past, after *or* later than

This informal preposition is mainly used in UK English to state:

That a certain time had already passed (It is **gone** my normal bedtime).

That a time is after a specific time (It must be **gone** 11 am already).

That it is later than (It is **gone** way past the time she normally gets home).

Take care not to confuse this with the past participle of the verb go (He has **gone** to work already).

Categories

Time

It was **gone** noon when he arrived.
The time is just **gone** 7 p.m.

Notes

IN

Inside an unsealed place *or* within a time

The primary use of this common preposition is to indicate being within an enclosure that is not completely sealed, for example a room with the door open – use **inside** if the door is closed. Other uses include:

Be contained by (I put it **in** a box)

Be surrounded by (She is walking **in** the park)

Be part of (He is **in** the team that will play on Saturday)

Be a member of (I have been given membership **in** the club)

Having an involvement (He took part **in** the marathon).

Pertain to a particular thing (My students all got a good mark **in** their English exams).

Be immediately after a period of time (I will let you know the results **in** a week or so).

Be within a certain time constraint (I will be working at home **in** the afternoon on that day)

Indicate by virtue of – note that it precedes a clause (She feels she will get a good grade **in** that she studied hard beforehand)

To indicate an order or arrangement (He put all his toys **in** a line on the floor)

To show activity during certain periods of time (He works at night and sleeps **in** the daytime)

To indicate a method – note that it precedes an infinitive (Are you coming **in** to work by car tomorrow?)

To give a reason for an action (She shook her head **in** sorrow).

To indicate a language or script (The book was written **in** English).

To indicate a tone (It is played **in** C#)

To indicate how something was delivered (She spoke **in** a quiet voice).

To indicate someone's personal standing (He has a friend **in** me).

To indicate the method of moving towards the present position (He is coming **in** a taxi).

There are also adjective versions of this word meaning: having an elected position (He has been **in** office for about a year) and being currently fashionable (It is the **in** thing at the moment).

There is also an adverb version (Come **in**!)

IN

Categories

Direction

Come **in** the study it is quiet there.
You must pay a congestion charge when you drive **in** London.

Place

I am currently stuck **in** a traffic jam.
I live **in** Bangkok.

Cause

She caused problems at work **in** her refusal to help out with the rush order.
The new product caused an increase **in** the company's profits.

Content

Do you have this **in** black?
She can still fit **in** the dress she wore as a teenager.

Time

We are going on holiday **in** April.
The peace movement was at its height **in** the 1960s.

Manner

He prefers speaking in French when he's **in** Canada.
This form needs to be completed **in** black ink.

Comparison

The prices had to be increased **in** order to restore profitability.
He prefers living **in** the country.

Notes

INSIDE

The inner part, space or side of something enclosed

Use this preposition to talk about:

The interior of something (I left it **inside** my car)

The closest point to the centre (The bulls-eye is **inside** the middle ring on a dart board)

A specific point of reference (He has a job **inside** the main ministry building).

It can also be used to **refer to something that is completely enclosed** (I put the letter **inside** this envelope), rather than use **in**, which generally refers to either a contained destination (I put it **in** the box), for referring to moving from the outside (She came **in** the room) or for referring to something that is contained in something that is open (I am **in** the room with the door open).

So use this preposition when talking about enclosing something.

There is an adverb version of this word (Come **inside**) and an adjective (The **inside** wall of the house was cracked)

There is also a noun version (The spy was on the **inside** of the agency).

Difference between INSIDE and IN

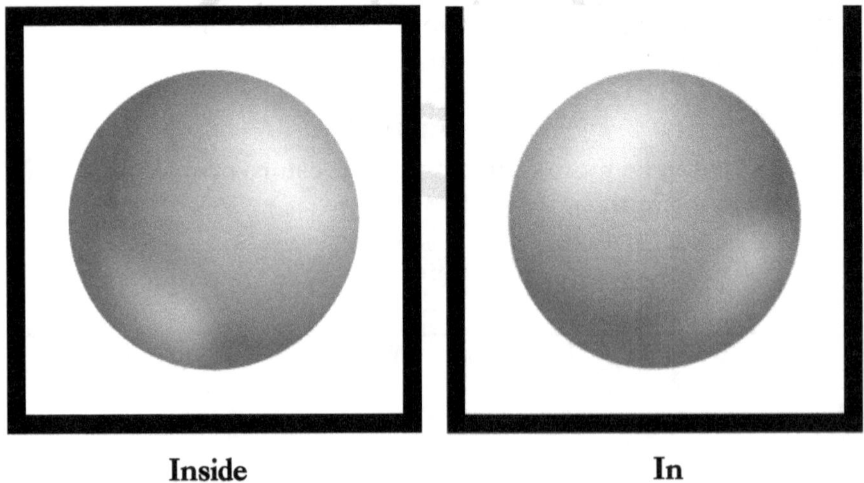

Inside   In

INSIDE

Categories

Direction

Can I put my coat **inside** the closet?
How do I get **inside** this building?

Place

There's a lot of room **inside** my new car.
The police think the murder took place **inside** the house.

Cause

I'm late because I left my car keys **inside** my locked car.
I forgot to put my parking permit **inside** my windscreen (US: Windshield)

Content

The instructions are **inside** the box.
Make sure you put plenty of padding **inside** the carton.

Time

He completed the marathon **inside** 3 hours.
You need to finish the exam **inside** the allotted time.

Manner

My teenaged daughter locks herself away **inside** her room for hours at a time.
She felt empty **inside** her heart after her husband died.

Comparison

It's warmer **inside** the car than out in the wind.
It is cooler in the street than **inside** my house.

Notes

INTO

Move towards the inside or middle of something

Use this preposition for describing the following:

Describe going inside of somewhere (She came **into** the room just after me).

Describe going to a geographic region (I am just turning **into** your road).

Describe being against using force or violence (He got **into** a fight with the school bully).

Describe producing from something (I am making this wood **into** a table).

Describe becoming (She is turning **into** a really dreadful person).

To indicate the time from the start of (It was about ten minutes **into** our flight when the fire started).

Describe being very interested in (He has immersed himself deeply **into** his new hobby).

Describe being attracted to (She is really **into** her new boyfriend).

To say how something will proceed (We are going **into** the talks with an open mind - **go into** = phrasal verb).

Describe being unwilling to clarify something (I am not going **into** the reasons for our decision).

Describe an unwillingness to discuss something (I am not going **into** that right now).

To indicate a mathematical divisor (2 goes **into** 8 four times).

Describe investigating something (The police are looking **into** how the crime was carried out).

Describe moving inwards towards a goal (I considering getting **into** a career in web design).

The main reason for using this preposition rather than **in**, is for **describing movement, action or change.**

It is only ever used as a preposition.

INTO

Categories

Direction

What's the best way of getting **into** the city centre? (US: center)
Is this the way **into** the building?

Place

She liked looking **into** his eyes.
As you move further **into** the park you'll enjoy how peaceful it is.

Cause

I got **into** electronics when I was a kid.
Dropping my phone in the toilet turned it **into** a piece of junk.

Content

I'm turning my house **into** apartments.
I'm changing **into** some dry clothes.

Manner

My daughter changed **into** a lovely young woman when she hit 20.
He turned **into** a recluse when his wife died.

Comparison

I have no idea what got **into** him, he used to be such a nice young man.
I'm not sure I like that he turned his car **into** a street racer.

Notes

LACKING

A shortage of

This word is commonly referred to in dictionaries as an adjective; however, it can be used as a preposition:

To indicate that there is a shortage of something (**Lacking** enough parts we had to improvise).

To show a complete absence of something (**Lacking** a vital component the workers were sent home)

It could be replaced with the preposition **without** in the context of having none of the particular thing. **Lacking** adds more nuance in that it indicates that **there may not be enough of something but there may still be a small quantity available.**

The adjective version means deficient in (Her appetite for adventure is **lacking**).

Categories

Content

Lacking moral fibre he fled at the first sound of gunfire.
Lacking choices she decided to cooperate.

Notes

　　Website: www.englishbook.shop

LESS

Not including

This preposition is used:

To indicate that something is not included (The computers were shipped **less** an operating system).

To indicate something being removed (Now add up the numbers **less** the number you first thought of).

It is most commonly used as a comparative adjective meaning that there are not as many (There are **less** people here than I thought) or being of lower importance (He is **less** qualified than her); whereas, the preposition essentially means none at all.

It can be replaced with the more formal preposition **excluding**.

Categories

Content

It costs $100 **less** tax.
The item is shipped **less** batteries.

Notes

LIKE

Similar to

This preposition is used for:

Indicating strong similarities in people (She looks a lot **like** her mother)

Simile to indicate that something that is somewhat similar to something else (This steak tastes **like** shoe leather).

To state that something is reminiscent of a place (This place is **like** the place we went on holiday to last year)

To state that something is reminiscent of an object (This car drives **like** the car I had twenty years ago).

There is a verb version of this word (I **like** ice cream), an adjective version (Mensa is a club containing **like**-minded people), a noun version (The place was filled with crooks, gangsters and the **like**), and a conjunction (It looks **like** the judge is returning to the court now).

It can also be used, in idiomatic English, as an intensifier (It was, **like**, awesome!) and to give approximations (there were **like** a hundred people at the party).

Categories

Comparison

She looks just **like** her mother.
I bought another car just **like** my old one.

Manner

It looks **like** the kind of storm we had last year.
It's not **like** you to be so studious.

Notes

MID

In the middle of

This rarely used preposition, which is often prefaced with an 'a' (**amid**), is used:

To indicate what something, or somebody, is surrounded by (It was a quiet place to think **mid** the bustling city)

To indicate being surrounded by (I couldn't hear what she was saying **mid** the noise in the canteen)

To be in the centre of something (We set up a stall **mid** the other market traders).

In most circumstances it can be replaced by **amidst** or **in the middle of.**

It is often used, with a prefix, to create an adjective that is used, with or without a hyphen, to indicate the middle of something (I had my **mid**morning coffee – without a hyphen - *or* I went to the **mid**-summer dance - hyphenated).

It is an old fashioned term and is mostly used in a literary sense, for example in novels.

Categories

Place

Did you see him **mid** the crowd?
He was like a rock **mid** all the turmoil.

Notes

MINUS

Reduce by a stated amount *or* be without

This preposition is used:

To indicate that something is lacking (I left home **minus** my umbrella)

To indicate that something has been taken away (I got a refund **minus** the tax).

It can also be used as an adjective to state that something is below a particular value (It was **minus** 5 ºC today).

Note: some grammarians suggest that when this word is used to indicate a mathematic function (ten **minus** two equals eight) then it is a noun; however, it can be used to preface a <u>noun clause</u> (This is what I owe **minus** <u>what I have already paid</u>) so it acts more like a preposition.

Categories

Content

What is 27.3 **minus** 12.7?
We seem to be **minus** some of our members today.

Comparison

It's just like England **minus** the rain.
He looks like his dad **minus** the beard.

Notes

NEAR

Not far away

Use this preposition for:

Describing something that, or someone who, is close to (My house is **near** the beach)

To describe something that is close proximity to (He came and stood **near** me)

To be somewhere around a certain time (It was **near** ten am when he finally arrived).

To indicate a capability (Her voice is **near** equal to Maria Callas).

It can be replaced in most cases with **close to.**

There are also an adjective version of this word (It is a **near** copy), a prefix version that combines with an adjective or a noun to produce something that almost happened (In the **near**-future *or* it was a **near**-miss), a noun version, with an idiomatic use meaning slightly rude (Lady Chatterley's lover was considered to be a bit **near**), and a verb version (As we **neared** the harbour a storm sprang up).

Categories

Place

We are **near** my house.
The hotel is **near** the highway.

Time

I will be leaving **near** five p.m.
It must be getting **near** your birthday.

Manner

No-one comes **near** her wit.
No-one has **near** her capabilities.

NEAR TO

Be in close proximity to a time or a place

This preposition is used:

To indicate being close to some place (We live **near to** the beach)

To indicate that something is close to something abstract (What she said was very **near to** the truth).

To indicate the current time is close to a specific known time (He arrived **near to** the time we usually eat supper).

It differs slightly from '**near**' as it implies being closer in position and is also used as a comparative to state being even closer (It was **near to** the place I ate lunch).

Near is more commonly used in US English and **near to** is more common in UK English.

Replacement: **Close to** has a very similar meaning

Categories

Place

It was **near to** that restaurant we ate at last week.
He got a ticket as he had parked **near to** the fire hydrant.

Time

The time of the meeting is **near to** the CEO's live web-cast.
It's **near to** that time (UK idiomatic use meaning it is close to the time to go home).

Notes

NEXT TO

Beside, alongside *or* in a sequence

Use this preposition for:

Being beside (I am standing **next to** her in the photograph).

Being alongside (I walked **next to** the wall as it's shadow made it cooler).

Immediately preceding in a sequence - usually referring to the penultimate/one before last position (I was **next to** last in the exam).

Following in a sequence (Who is that **next to** the first guy on the left?)

In US English sometimes '**next**' would be used rather than '**next to**'.

It can be replaced with **beside**.

Categories

Place

We live **next to** the harbour.
The motel is **next to** the highway.

Notes

Reference

OF

Possession, belonging *or* origin

Use this commonly used preposition for expressing the following:

Describing a point in time - for example **ten 'o' clock** - where 'o' is an abbreviation of **'of the…'**

Supplying a date (It is the 2nd **of** May

Describing qualities (She has a heart **of** gold).

Describing characteristics (It has the strength **of** steel and the lightness **of** aluminium).

Describing composition (It is comprised **of** layers **of** fabric).

Describing the original substance (It is made **of** silicon).

Describing the geographical origin (He was called John **of** Gaunt).

Describing the separate parts (It is made **of** three separate parts).

Granting a distinction (She is the bride's maid **of** honour).

Describing owner of a possession (That dog **of** his is noisy).

Clarifying the agency (He is head **of** the HR section).

Giving the cause (The direction **of** the wind was pushing us forwards).

It can also be used for referring to:

A part of a whole (Partitive effect – e.g. Some **of** us like classical music)

And for introducing a subject matter (Darwin wrote the Origin **of** Species).

Another use is in expressing the object of an activity or state ("objective genitive") by using one noun to express the ownership of something represented by a <u>head noun</u> that then acts like an intransitive verb (His <u>love</u> **of** his country is obvious *or* The <u>fear</u> **of** death is in all of us).

Note this latter use derived from Latin and is not as common as it was; nowadays, we use a simpler structure (”The <u>fear</u> **of** death is in all of us” is now “ We all fear death”).

In many circumstances we can replace the word with **from**.

Categories

Direction (origin)

Henry the eight's first wife was called Catherine **of** Aragon.
Men **of** Kent are different to Kentish men and I can't remember why.

Place

The house is within walking distance **of** the train station.
I live on the outskirts **of** London.

Cause

He died **of** liver failure.
He is the cause **of** his mother's grief.

Content

He is friend **of** mine.
It is made **of** silk.

Manner

He has the brain **of** a genius.
She is the most thoughtful **of** people.

Comparison

He is one **of** the best engineers I know.
The worst entertainment **of** all was the karaoke.

Time

It's the twelfth **of** November today.
We get paid on the first **of** the month.

Notes

OFF

Away from a place, state or position *or* not connected

This preposition is used for the following:

To indicate movement away from a position (The aircraft was drifting **off** course because of an instrument failure).

To no longer have possession of (My IPad was stolen **off** me last week)

To be away from (We live a long way **off** the highway)

To state something is not on (I turned **off** the air-conditioner as it was getting too cold)

To be disconnected (I logged **off** the Internet before starting work)

To subtract from (I bought the new computer as I got 20% **off** the normal price). Note this could be an absolute amount ($10) or a relative amount (10%).

To be distant from (You need to turn **off** the main road just after the post office)

To be no longer wanting (She had gone **off** her new boyfriend as he was so childish)

To be not taking or consuming (The new born lamb is **off** its feed).

To be placed after a number of parts in a whole – like a delivery (We shipped 27 **off** clutch plates with the order - 27 off = 27 pieces).

This word can also be used as a verb – meaning to kill in a pre-meditated way (He was **offed** by a mafia hit-man).

There is also an adverb version (Our destination is five miles **off**).

It can also be used as adjective (Have you turned it **off**?), but it is often confused with the preposition.

The easiest way to determine whether it is an adjective or a preposition is to look for a <u>preceding</u> article or determiner – in which case it is an adjective, for example 'I have **an off** road 4X4' – where **off** is an adjective as it is preceded by '**an**'; whereas, 'I drove **off the** road' – **off** is a preposition because '**the**' is after the word.

OFF

Categories

Direction

You need to go **off** the main road to get to his farm
Get **off** the freeway at the next junction.

Place

There are probably other life-forms **off** in a distant galaxy.
Malta is a small island **off** the coast of Sicily.

Cause

He is way **off** finishing his part of the project.
He is better now, so he can come **off** the tablets.

Manner

He was very **off** with me.
She said she'd gone **off** me, so I guess she doesn't like me any more.

Comparison

There is 10% **off** the price of this shirt.
You usually get money **off** the usual price if you haggle.

Notes

Reference

ON

In a position above and touching *or* included in *or* at a date *or* connected

This is a very commonly used preposition with the following uses:

To describe an elevated position (I put it **on** the shelf).

To give a date for a forthcoming event (The match is scheduled to take place **on** Monday)

To say something is on the upper surface of (My keys are **on** the table).

To be touching from above (The candles were placed **on** the cake).

To be covered by (She put **on** her coat over her clothes).

To be at the date of (She was born **on** the first of May).

To be sometime during the day of (I will see you sometime **on** Saturday).

To be dealing with the subject of (He is giving a speech **on** software engineering).

To describe what something is about (I read a book **on** Roman history).

To be concerning something (Have you got any information **on** fixing washing machines?)

To be touching or wearing (She is wearing a cute hat **on** her head).

To be hanging from (There is a spider's web **on** the ceiling).

To be paid for by (The drinks are **on** me as I just won the lottery).

To be in the possession of (Have you got a penknife **on** you?).

To indicate a means of subsistence (I am living **on** less than $1 a day).

To give a reason (He was arrested **on** suspicion of corruption).

To explain why (She bought a new pair of shoes **on** a whim).

To use to pay (He put the bill **on** his credit card).

To describe immediately preceding event (The students left **on** finishing the exam).

To assume a reason (You did that **on** purpose).

To indicate a medium (There was a good program **on** the television).

To indicate a way of doing something (I will talk to her **on** the telephone)

To give a reason for being away (He is overseas **on** business)

To be occupied with (The detective is working **on** a case).

To give reason for present status (The building is **on** fire)

ON

Uses continued...

To give a reason for non-availability (It is **on** its scheduled maintenance)

To regularly take a drug or medicine (He is **on** medication for his cold).

To be supported by (You should stand **on** a chair to reach the light).

There are also adverb (Can you please turn the light **on**) and adjective (I couldn't quite reach the **on** switch) versions of this word.

Categories

Direction

You need to go **on** bus number 82.
He will be getting **on** the flight about now.

Place

The books are **on** the table.
There is a mobile phone mast **on** my house

Cause

The company said they'd issue a statement **on** the cause of the oil spill.
He's crazy; he spends all his money **on** gambling.

Content

My mobile went dead **on** me.
There are no ethnic minorities **on** the committee.

Manner

He's been quiet since he's been working **on** his new book.
I store my work **on** my flash drive.

Comparison

I couldn't improve **on** the offer she made.
Profits are up **on** last year's.

Time

What are you doing **on** Friday?
My birthday is **on** the 12th of November

NOTWITHSTANDING

Despite (formal)

This preposition is very similar to the preposition **despite;** in fact, in general correspondence **despite** is more commonly used. **Notwithstanding** is regarded as a 'weaker' preposition than **despite** and would commonly be used when granting or pleading for concessions even though there may be obstacles.

Use this preposition for formal documents:

To describe why there was reluctance to impose something (**Notwithstanding** your plea for leniency the crime is too serious to warrant anything other than a custodial sentence - note: most likely spoken by a judge).

To acknowledge differences but still be willing to reach an agreement (We signed the contract **notwithstanding** the unresolved issues).

To acknowledge that a previous agreement exists but still asking for changes (We would like to vary the terms of the contract **notwithstanding** <u>that it still has two years to run</u> - note: <u>clause</u>).

To be a more polite way of asking for concessions (I beg you to release me from my debt **notwithstanding** the amount owed).

In legal texts it could be replaced with **even if.**

Categories

Comparison

They made good progress **notwithstanding** the foul weather.
Notwithstanding the evidence, the jury has still not reached a verdict.

Manner

Notwithstanding our different views we have made good progress.
Notwithstanding the obstacles I see us reaching an agreement.

ONTO

Allow movement to and on a particular place

Use this preposition for:

To desire a change of topic (We need to move **onto** the next item on the agenda).

To describe moving up (My office has been moved **onto** the top floor).

To describe a change in circumstances (I was put **onto** a higher salary band).

To get on a method of transportation (She was just getting **onto** the bus when her phone rang).

To place in a high position (He moved the book **onto** a higher shelf).

It is **primarily used to describe movement**; whereas, **on** is used to describe something static.

This word can be replaced with the preposition **upon** in most circumstances.

Categories

Direction

You need to get **onto** the bus now or it'll leave without you.
The containers are currently being loaded **onto** the ship.

Place

Put the groceries **onto** the counter and I'll put them away.
Climb **onto** the couch and I'll examine you.

Content

He changed the topic of conversation **onto** a less contentious one.
How did we get **onto** this subject anyway?

Manner

Don't get **onto** your high horse (idiom = act in a morally superior way)
She did everything she could to hold **onto** her man.

OPPOSITE

Position facing but from the other side

This preposition is used:

To describe something or someone that is facing someone or something else (She is sitting **opposite** me).

To be across from (My house is on the **opposite** side of the road from the shop).

To act with (He has played **opposite** many famous actresses).

To be in a contrary position (He took an **opposite** position on the issue to the rest of the team).

It could be replaced by **on the other side of** in most circumstances.

This word is most commonly used as an adjective (She is the **opposite** sex to me)

It can also be used as an adverb (You know the factory? Well, I live **opposite**).

It can also be used as a noun (His twin brother was his **opposite**).

It was derived from the Latin verb 'oppono' meaning 'being opposed to'.

Categories

Direction

You need to go in the **opposite** direction to where you're facing.
Turn left **opposite** the post office.

Place

I live **opposite** the student dormitories.
They sat **opposite** each other over the lunch table.

Comparison

What's the **opposite** of inflammable?
I like to sit **opposite** the window, not with my back to it.

OUT

Show movement away from inside a place

This preposition is most commonly used:

To describe movement away from the inside (He went **out** the door)

To go away from the centre (It spun **out** of position after coming loose).

To go from inside (She went **out** the door).

It can be replaced with the word **from** to describe general movement away from somewhere.

There are also adjective version of this word (You were **out** when I called) and an adverb ("Get **out!**" she shouted).

There is also a verb version (He was **outed** as a spy by the agency)

And a noun version (He was given an **out** by the umpire)

Categories

Direction

He jumped **out** the window to escape from the fire.
My groceries fell **out** my bag when the strap broke.

Notes

OUT OF

Away from the origin or desired position

Even though this preposition consists of two other prepositions it is used as one word (separated by a space) and is commonly used for expressing the following:

To talk about someone going from the inside to the outside of somewhere (He rushed **out of** the door).

To describe something being removed from (I took it **out of** the box).

To describe having emerged from (He came **out of** his coma last night).

To state the motivation for doing something (I gave her the money **out of** pity for her).

To give the reason for not being a part of something (He was left **out of** the party as he was feeling unwell).

To describe being without (I have run **out of** money – **run out of** = phrasal verb)

To be no longer in possession of (We have run **out of** free books)

To not having more (I have run **out of** things to do to stop myself getting bored).

To become divested of (I got **out of** investing in equities due to the stock market instability).

To give the reason for not being in a customary state (They suddenly went **out of** business)

To give a reason for not being in a desired state (I'm sorry we have to stop as we have run **out of** time).

To describe the original material (It is made **out of** cotton).

To express a fraction (Only one student finished on time **out of** the whole class).

To state a ratio (Less that 1 **out of** a 1,000 people has ever stopped smoking using nicotine patches).

In certain circumstances it can be replaced with **from inside of** – for expressing movement or **not part of** – for expressing something outside the norm.

Note that this preposition is actually more prevalent than using the preposition **out** on its own, as **out** tends to be used more as an adverb than a preposition.

OUT OF

Categories

Direction

Go **out of** the gate, turn left and you'll see it on your right.
You'll need to go **out of** the city to find a genuine farm shop.

Cause

No coffee today, I'm afraid, as the machine is **out of** order.
The boxer lost the fight as he was **out of** condition.

Content

This dress is made **out of** pure Thai silk.
Don created a great deal of fuss **out of** the fact he had a PHD.

Manner

I bought the computer **out of** my pay.
He had to settle the tax bill **out of** his savings.

Comparison

I prefer products made **out of** natural materials.
Eight **out of** ten students have trouble with prepositions.

Time

We ran **out of** time.
The restaurant did an **out of** hours take out service.

Idiomatic

I am feeling **out of** sorts (UK English meaning ill).
What he did was **out of** character (Outside his normal behaviour).

Notes

OUTSIDE

Be away from within a place *or* away from the norm

Use this preposition to describe the following:

To say something or someone is near but not in (The restaurant is **outside** the office building on the other side of the street)

Say something or someone is apart from (He was **outside** the house when it happened).

To say something or someone is not within but close by (I managed to park **outside** the office).

To say something is away from the norm (This is **outside** my normal line of work - not what I'd usually do).

There is a lot of confusion with the adverb version of this word. The rule is that if the sentence can still make grammatical sense without the single word **outside** (I ran **outside** – where '**I ran**' can stand alone) then it is an adverb; whereas, if it precedes a noun phrase or clause it is a preposition (I am outside <u>the coffee shop</u> - <u>noun phrase</u> - I am outside *<u>that coffee shop you told me about</u>* - <u>noun clause</u>).

There are also adjective (They called in an **outside** expert) and noun versions (The house is great inside but the **outside** is ugly).

It may be replaced with **away from** in most instances.

Categories

Direction

You need to go **outside** the building to smoke.
I went to the coffee shop **outside** the office.

Place

Outside the park there is a wilderness.
His secretary has a desk **outside** his office.

Manner

Outside his work he leads a lonely life.
We need to think **outside** the box (outside the box = not rely on previous experience or current thinking).

OUTSIDE OF

Except *or* apart from

This compound preposition is used:

To describe exceptions (**Outside of** the people here present is anyone interested in this proposal?).

To describe being apart from (He wasn't comfortable doing anything **outside of** his normal experience).

To describe being away from (It was **outside** of anything I had seen before).

It can also be used in place of, or be replaced by, the preposition **besides** (No-one else came **outside of** the regular customers / No-one else came **besides** the regular customers).

Categories

Place

He had no interests **outside of** his work.
Outside of the office there is a huge car park.

Manner

I work on my book **outside of** my normal office hours.
He acted **outside of** his normal moral standards.

Comparison

Outside of this office the world is not insane.
Outside of her profession she is not very capable.

Notes

OVER

Above, higher than or across from something else

This preposition can be used:

To describe things that are more than desired (That item is **over** the price I am willing to pay)

To describe moving across an intervening space (She came **over** the bridge to see us).

To say that something is not understood – idiomatic use (Particle physics is way **over** my head).

To describe something that covers something else (the cover **over** my bike saved it from getting wet).

To describe something happening for the whole duration of something (My friends stayed with us **over** the weekend).

To go across (We need a footbridge **over** the busy road).

To span (They built a flyover **over** the river).

To be in excess of (I think I am **over** the limit for driving).

To divide by (4 **over** 2 = 2).

To compare with (Votes are up **over** the last election).

To be finally finished with (I think she is **over** her ex-boyfriend).

To state a reason (I am rather angry **over** your remark).

To have overcome (I think we have got **over** the problems we've been having since the software update).

To cross a barrier by going up then down (The dog jumped **over** the fence).

It differs from the preposition 'above' in that 'over' generally means that something is moving.

The word may be replaced by **above** or **in excess of** depending on the context.

This word is also commonly used as an adverb (It flew **over** *or* it is **over**).

There is also an adjective version (The harvest is over, now we can relax).

In UK English there is a noun version used in cricket to denote that six balls have been played (That is the end of the fifth **over**).

Note: **overtime** is a noun.

OVER

Categories

Direction

It's just **over** there.
To see the answers turn **over** the page (turn over = phrasal verb).

Cause

They hated living apart as they could only talk **over** the phone.
I can't buy a car **over** that price as I don't want to borrow money.

Content

It took me a while to get **over** dengue fever.
There is no point arguing **over** something so trivial.

Manner

She didn't like having a woman boss **over** her.
Her boyfriend was all **over** her.

Comparison

Most of the books are **over** $20.
The department has spent $25,000 **over** their budget.

Time

Premium beef gets better **over** time.
I'm working **over** the lunch break.

Notes

OWING TO

Because of *or* on account of

Use this preposition:

To state the reason for something not happening (The parade has been cancelled **owing to** the bad weather)

To give the reason for some measure having to be taken (**Owing to** certain people abusing the system it has been shut down until further notice).

This preposition is a more formal way of saying **because of** and tends to be used in professional communications.

It can be replaced with **because of** in most instances or when a less formal preposition is needed.

Categories

Cause

The concert was cancelled **owing to** the lack of ticket sales.
Owing to the lack of a quorum, the committee couldn't pass the vote.

Notes

Website: www.englishbook.shop

PACE

With all due respect for/to

This preposition is very formal and tends to get used mainly in legal texts and official documents.

It is used:

To express polite disagreement (**Pace** my learned friend's remarks I beg to disagree).

To express a contradiction to what has been said (I think you will find, **pace** your opening statement, that the facts do not comport with your views).

It doesn't have a direct replacement the nearest match being **notwithstanding**.

It is more commonly used as a noun (A **pace** is usually understood to be 2.5 feet long) or a verb (You will need to **pace** yourself if you want to finish the marathon).

Categories

Comparison

Pace popular opinion, he isn't as stupid as he looks.
The world, **pace** the doom mongers, is not getting poorer.

Notes

PAST

A position, quantity or time beyond a particular point

This preposition can be used:

To state that something is beyond a limit (The number of people attending is **past** the maximum number).

To go beyond a position (You need to turn left **past** the post office).

To go beyond a time (The show starts at half **past** 6).

It can also be used in the past tense, **to say something has already moved beyond** (He went **past** me at 100 km/h) or is going to move beyond (We will go **past** the lighthouse to enter the harbour).

There are adjective (Over the **past** day or so), adverb (He went **past**) and noun (He was always talking about the **past**) versions of this word.

Note that, even though it was derived from the past tense of the verb 'pass' it no longer is used in that way; the past participle of the verb 'pass' is now **passed**.

Categories

Direction

Go **past** the library and up the hill.
You have just gone **past** the turning.

Place

He went **past** the champion on the last lap.
I think he drove **past** us a few minutes ago

Time

It is now half **past** three.
He is **past** the age where he cares about what he wears.

Notes

PENDING

One thing must wait until another thing happens

Use this preposition:

Give the reason why something cannot happen until something else has happened (The project has been put on hold **pending** a review).

To give a reason for a delay (Your pass has been held up **pending** authorisation).

There is an adjective version of this word (he has a patent **pending**) in common use.

Categories

Time

All courses are suspended **pending** a review by the academic committee. They were left waiting **pending** the boss's decision.

Notes

PER

For expressing rates, prices or measurements *or* a fixed method

Use this preposition:

To supply a rate (My car does 10 kilometres **per** litre)

To give an interval (One tablet **per** day after meals).

To state an individual cost (The tickets cost $5 **per** person).

To give instructions for the administration of medicine - by way of (The pills should be administered **per** os - by mouth).

To state that something is in accordance with (I assembled the table **per** the instructions).

This word is most commonly used to express a proportion as part of one hundred (100 **per**cent) most commonly found in things like interest rates.

Percent is abbreviated with the symbol **%** - **cent** means one hundred.

Depending on the context it may be replaced with **for each, to each, every, of** or **according to**.

Categories

Comparison

The apples are $2:50 **per** kilo.
The meal is $5 **per** person.

Manner

We must act **per** the instructions
I need you to deliver in batches **per** my purchase order

Notes

PLUS

In addition to

Many grammar books list this word purely as a conjunction rather than a preposition, but it is used in prepositional phrases so it is listed here.

It is mainly used to provide inclusions (There are fifteen people on the bus **plus** the driver).

There are also noun (having experience in this area is a **plus**) and adjective (He has many **plus** points) versions of this word.

It can also be used as a conjunction (I got a good salary **plus** I was given a company car) and a conjunctive adverb (You will need to bring a change of clothes; **plus**, you will need to provide a packed lunch).

The phrase **in addition to** can be used instead.

Categories

Content

Both parents are going **plus** their three children.
I'll have the soup **plus** the fish.

Comparison

What is two hundred and thirty two **plus** nine hundred and six?
The cost is $100 **plus** sales tax.

Notes

Reference

POST

After

This preposition is mainly used to indicate being after some event. It is regarded as a stronger word than **after** as it is mainly used **to denote a significant event that has long-term, usually irreversible, effects.**

Use this preposition to show:

Being later in time (P.M. is an abbreviation of **Post** Meridiem meaning 'after midday' or 'after noon').

Being later in order (The house is an example of **post** modern architecture).

It is often used as a prefix followed by a hyphen (**post -**).

The most common use of the word is as a verb meaning to display publicly (He **posted** a message on the Internet), to send (She **posted** a letter to her friend) or to assign (He was **posted** to the embassy in Karachi).

There are also noun versions (Most Jewish houses have a Mezuzah affixed to the door **post**) or to refer to the postal service (I sent it by **post**).

Categories

Time

The Mad Max movies are set in a **post** apocalyptic world.
They were suffering **post** match blues after their team lost.

Notes

PRECEDING/PRE

Just before in time or position

This preposition is mainly used to indicate being before some event. It is regarded as a stronger word than **before** as it is mainly used to denote a significant event that has already occurred or is likely to occur and it refers to the long-term, usually irreversible, effects. It takes two forms: the more formal **preceding** and the abbreviated **pre**. When it is used to denote the position it is used to denote something that is moving; whereas, **before** is used to refer to something that is not moving.

Use this preposition to show:

Just before in time (The chairman will give a speech to the staff **preceding** him addressing the board meeting).

Just before in position (**Preceding** her husband she entered the restaurant).

State of being earlier in time than some event (The new teacher was suffering **pre** class nerves).

Pre is sometimes used in colloquial English instead of **preceding** (We will create the design specification **pre** the design meeting).

It is commonly used as a prefix followed by a hyphen (**pre -**)

It can be replaced with **prior to** in most circumstances

Categories

Time

He is doing his **pre** match exercises.
They signed a **pre** nuptial agreement.

Place

He like to walk **preceding** his staff.
Protocol dictates that senior officials enter the chamber **preceding** their staff.

PRO

In favour of *or* having a positive view about

Use this preposition **to show being in favour of something** (He is **pro** social housing).

There are also noun version of this word, meaning doing something for money (He is a tennis **pro**)

An adjective version (There was an overwhelming **pro** vote).

And an adverb version (Are you **pro** or anti?).

It is commonly used as a hyphenated prefix (I am **pro-**democracy).

It can be replaced with **for** or **in favour of**.

Categories

Manner

Libertarians are **pro** freedom.
The lawyer took the case **pro** bono meaning he did it for free.

Notes

                    Website: www.englishbook.shop

QUA

In the capacity of

This word is primarily use in formal documents or statements. It is not used very often.

Many grammar books list this word purely as a conjunction rather than a preposition, but it is used in prepositional phrases so it is listed here.

It is mainly used to show in what capacity someone is acting (The partners **qua** owners are responsible for any liabilities).

It could be replaced by **as being** or **in the capacity of**.

It was derived from the Latin word **qui** meaning **who**.

Categories

Comparison

The beneficiaries **qua** executors should attend the will reading.
The actor **qua** the leading man was paid a lot of money.

Notes

RE

About (Formal)

Use this preposition for the following:

To show what this document is in reference to (I am providing this statement **re** the letter of complaint you sent)

To provide a link to previous correspondence - usually at the top of a formal business letter (**Re:** Your letter inst. delivery problems - note inst. means within this month).

It is usually followed by a colon (**re:**)

Categories

Content

Re our discussion I am now in a position to address your concerns. Can you supply an update **re** the expected delivery date?

Notes

REGARDING

Paying particular notice to

This word is used:

To refer to something else that has relevance (We need a chat **regarding** the differences in the old and new contracts).

To state what something is about (I need to see you **regarding** the email you sent).

It is also very close in meaning to the preposition, **concerning**; however, **regarding** is used to imply that the matter is not urgent or of concern, whereas **concerning** means that it may be serious.

This preposition may be replaced with **about** or **in reference to** depending on the context.

Note: there is a shortened version of this preposition **Re** which is used mainly in business correspondence - as shown on the previous page. Either can be used; however, **re** tends to be used as a heading in a business letter and **regarding** tends to be used in the main body text.

Categories

Content

The boss made a decision **regarding** my pay raise.
The criminal was questioned **regarding** his alibi for the night of the robbery.

Notes

ROUND

In a circular direction *or* around to the other side

This preposition is often used in place of the word **around** when talking about close approximations or near estimates in particular with the word **about** (It is **round about** 30 degrees today) and is mainly used in the UK.

It can also be used:

To describe moving in a circular motion (My dog is running **round** the garden).

To describe somewhere that is on the other side of something and therefore out of sight (I parked **round** the back).

There are adjective version of this word (The **round** ball)

And an adverb version (Instead of asking her to move he went **round**)

Plus a noun version (The next **round** of the match).

And, finally, a verb version (He **rounded** the corner and hit a tree).

It can be replaced with **to the back of** *or* **other side of.**

Categories

Direction

Run **round** the back and see if we left the window open.
Go **round** the corner and there it is.

Place

Is there much to do **round** here?
Last night we went **round** her house.

Content

That idea has being going **round** in my head.
The virus has gone **round** the office like wildfire.

Notes

SANS

Without (Formal)

This word is primarily use in formal documents or statements. There is also a French word **sans**, which has the same meaning. It is generally used in formal correspondence or speech to show that something is lacking or missing.

It is mainly used to show that something is missing that would normally be present (The product was delivered **sans** the invoice).

There is a French expression '**sans-culottes**' (meaning without trousers), which was a term used to refer to the common people in 18th century France. It is sometime used in English texts to disparagingly refer to the lower classes or to militant radicals.

It could be replaced by **without**.

It was derived from the Latin word **sine** meaning **without**.

Categories

Content

We had to start the performance **sans** the leading lady.
He bumbles through life **sans** common sense.

Notes

SAVE

Apart from

This preposition is used:

To single out someone who doesn't conform (They all brought pens **save** Emily)

To provide an exception (Everything is forbidden **save** where it is specifically allowed).

It is commonly collocated with **for** (I saw all of the animals **save for** the unicorn).

This word is mainly used in formal contexts, for informal sentences use the word **except**.

There are noun version of the word (it was a great **save** by the goalkeeper).

And a verb version (Do you **save** money every month?).

It can be replaced with the words **except** or **but**.

Categories

Content

I found them all, **save** one.
There was no-one there, **save for** old Fred.

Notes

SHORT

Deficient in

This preposition is used:

To indicate that there is a deficiency in something (The battalion was **short** sufficient artillery).

To indicate a negative position in finance (He was **short** the market prior to the closing bell).

It can be replaced by the preposition **lacking**.

It is commonly used as an adjective meaning lacking in height (My wife is very **short**), not having a long time (He had a **short** life), being more limited than expected (She wore a very **short** skirt), having a deficiency in one of the senses (He is **short** sighted) or being rude (she was very **short** with me this morning).

There is a singular noun version that means an accidental electrical contact (There is a **short** in the wiring somewhere) and a plural noun meaning trousers or pants that end before the knee (She was wearing a very skimpy pair of **shorts**).

The adverb version means in an abrupt way (He stopped **short** of the end of the pier) or be interrupted (He stopped her **short** before she gave away any secrets).

Categories

Content

The ship was **short** a chief engineer.
I am **short** the cash to buy it.

Notes

SINCE

From a specific time

This preposition is commonly used for **describing how long something has been happening for** and is commonly collocated with the perfect continuous verb form to **say when the action being described started** (I have been working here since October), note that it doesn't describe the length of time, you would use the preposition for to do that (I have been working here for six months).

It can also be used:

To say why something is true or has happened (I left without you **since** you weren't here on time).

To say that you haven't done something again after doing something (I haven't used calculus **since** I finished university).

It often precedes a time, day or date.

There is an adverb (I saw her last week and haven't seen her **since**) and conjunction (I haven't seen you **since** we were at school together) versions of this word.

It can be replaced in some instances with the word **from**. It replaced the (now) archaic preposition **sithence.**

Categories

Time

I've been waiting here **since** 1 p.m.
There hasn't been a snow storm here **since** 1998.

Idiomatic

Since when did you get to tell us what to do?
Since Nelson got his eye back. (UK English meaning it never happened).

Notes

THAN

To compare two or more things

This preposition is used **to introduce a comparison** and is usually associated with single word comparatives (She is **cleverer than** him), and suffix comparatives or adverbs such as:

More - he earns **more than** her - with no adjective but using the adverb **more** to compare the results of the verb **earn** - or she is **more** intelligent **than** him – with a compared result of the adjective **intelligent.**

Less - with uncountable nouns (she weighs **less than** him) and **fewer** - with countable nouns (**fewer** people came this year **than** last year).

It is mainly used in comparing the effect of adjectives on nouns or pronouns (example: *noun/pronoun* is more/less *adjective* **than** *noun/pronoun*).

It can be replaced with **compared to** in most instances.

There is a conjunction (I like this better **than** I like that one) version of this word, which is used to indicate preferences using clauses rather **than** prepositional phrases.

Categories

Comparison

Pi is bigger **than** 3 and smaller **than** 4
I'm taller **than** my daughter.

Place

My new house is bigger **than** my old house.
Thailand is larger **than** Cambodia.

Notes

THROUGH

From one end, or side, of something to the other

This preposition is mainly used:

To describe going from one side to another (He walked **through** the door)

To describe entering and then exiting (I went **through** the reception area on my way out of the building)

To describe moving while being surrounded (She enjoyed walking **through** the forest *or* I walked **through** the crowd)

To describe moving in and out of a situation (She avoided blame **through** not having been there at the time)

It can also be used to describe how something was achieved, for example; **by way of** (we expanded the business **through** a bank loan) or **by means of** (The gang got most of its money **through** extortion).

In the US it is also used to describe a set of inclusive dates, days or times (I worked from Monday **through** Friday) and is sometimes abbreviated as **thru.**

It can usually be replaced with **via** or **by way of.**

Categories

Direction

Go **through** that door over there and the toilets are on the left.
You'll have to go **through** the application procedure.

Cause

They lost the order **through** quality control problems.
I get a car **through** my work.

Manner

He failed the exam **through** laziness.
She succeeds in everything she does **through** sheer tenacity.

Place

He often went jogging **through** the park.
The shark glided effortlessly **through** the sea.

Time

He slept **through** his whole class this morning.
It rained **through** the night and into the morning.

THROUGHOUT

During a whole period of time *or* in every part of

This word has completely different meanings to the preposition **through** (see the previous page).

Use this preposition:

To refer to something that is in every part of something else (The bacteria quickly spread **throughout** the hospital)

To describe something being all through (the smell of fried food was there **throughout** the whole house).

To describe from the first part to the last part (He was talking **throughout** the ceremony).

It can be replaced in most instances with the word **during**.

There is an adverb version of this word (My car was cleaned **throughout**).

Categories

Time

He coughed **throughout** the concert.
She worked hard **throughout** her time at University.

Place

The flu virus spread **throughout** the department.
English is being learned **throughout** the whole world.

Notes

TILL

Up to *or* as late as

This preposition is commonly used:

To provide an end time (I worked **till** 6 p.m.).

To state a relative end point (We will continue **till** the next shift gets here).

To state that something may go on to an unknown point in the future (She has to work **till** the report is done).

It can be replaced by the preposition **until**. It is generally regarded as the abbreviation of **until** but it has no apostrophe and it has an additional 'l' there it should be regarded as a separate word.

There is a verb version of this word meaning to plough (The farmer **tills** his fields before sowing the seeds).

And a noun version meaning a place to keep money (Did you take some money from the **till**?).

Categories

Time

I will wait here **till** 1 p.m.
She lacked the energy to go on **till** the end of the marathon.

Idiomatic

We'll work **till** we drop.
You can wait **till** hell freezes over for me to pay you (meaning never).

Notes

TIMES

To multiply

This preposition is mainly used in stating the product is of multiplying two, or more, numbers (two **times** two is four).

It can also be used in an abstract sense to balance experiences (Happiness is the product of health **times** wealth, if your health is zero then it doesn't matter how much wealth you have).

It can be replaced with **multiplied by**.

There are noun version of this word (He is behind the **times**).

There is also a verb version (He **times** every event).

Categories

Content

$X_L = 2\pi fl$ which is 2 **times** 3.14 **times** the frequency **times** the inductor value.
The square of 2 (2^2) is 2 **times** 2.

Notes

TO

In the direction of a result

This is a very commonly used preposition, with the main use being **to indicate the direction or destination of someone or something.**

It is used:

To indicate the destination (I am going **to** the market).

To indicate the direction of something (The cat is moving **to** the fish tank).

To indicate the direction of someone (I am going **to** bed).

To say someone is going in (He went **to** the entrance)

To say someone or something is arriving at (He is coming directly **to** the office).

To clarify the indirect object (I gave the book **to** him).

To indicate result of action (She was scared **to** death of spiders).

To indicate purpose (I devote a lot time **to** my books).

To indicate a necessity (I am addicted **to** my early morning coffee).

Another common use is where it is used after certain adjectives to indicate their application, such as: **similar** (His coat is **similar to** mine), **relevant** (I am not sure the point you raised is **relevant to** the subject under discussion) and **pertinent** (I think what you did is pertinent **to** the charges that have been laid).

It can also be used with adjectives to point to the recipient of the adjective (I was kind **to** him *or* he was nasty **to** me).

Another common use is when **giving the time**, where it is used to state the number of minutes prior to the hour (The time is five **to** one) and to indicate ratios (The ratio of milk **to** water in the mixture is 5:1).

In mathematics it is used to **indicate that the preceding term is to be raised to the power of the following value** – e.g. exponentiation (Two squared is two **to** the power of two).

It can also be used to **indicate a range on inclusive numbers** (I chose numbers 1 **to** 5), days (I work Monday **to** Saturday) or dates (I will be in the US from the 2nd **to** the 5th of November).

A further use of this word is in infinitives where it precedes the bare – present simple – version of a verb.

Sometimes it may be replaced with **towards** *or* **in the direction of.**

TO

Categories

Direction

How do I get **to** the University from here?
You need to go **to** the post office to send that parcel.

Place

They stood back **to** back and faced the enemies surrounding them.
This car can do fifty miles **to** the gallon.

Cause

He's just found out he failed **to** his dismay.
I lent it **to** someone and they never gave it back.

Content

He does everything **to** a strict timetable.
It would be **to** your advantage if you studied more.

Time

I was studying from 2001 **to** 2006
There's only a week to go **to** the New Year.

Manner

He was really rude **to** me.
He is a consultant **to** the finance sector.

Comparison

Gasoline is really expensive compared **to** last year.
That's me, standing **to** the left of John, in that photograph.

Notes

TOWARD(S)

In the direction of *or* closer to

Note that in US English this word tends to be written as **toward**, with no suffixed **s**, and in UK English it is written as **towards**.

It has a number of meanings, such as:

To move in the direction of but not yet arrive (She is walking **towards** the door)

To provide feelings, such as emotional attachment or general thoughts, about someone (What are your feelings **towards** him?).

To give someone instructions on the forward direction they should take (You should study **towards** your goal of becoming a doctor).

To give a reason for a particular action (I am saving **towards** my holiday).

To state the location of something, relative to the present position and in the direction of the final goal (You need to walk **towards** the station and turn left at the traffic lights).

It can be replaced with **in the direction of** when talking about directions to a place.

Categories

Direction

I can see her walking **towards** me.
As you drive **towards** the town centre (US: center) it 's on your left.

Cause

We are all working **towards** a common goal.
I can study after my father gave me money **towards** the tuition fees.

Manner

She was always affectionate **towards** me.
He has a relaxed attitude **towards** his students.

Place

That's us the photograph, **towards** the back of the crowd.
The statue can be found **towards** the middle of the park.

Time

It's getting **towards** closing time.
It gets dark **towards** the middle of the afternoon in mid-winter.

TWIXT

Between (old formal, idiomatic or literary use only)

This preposition is used **to describe something that is between two, usually undesirable, things** (I was caught **twixt** my wife and my daughter).

It is generally regarded as old and rather formal and so it tends to be found mainly in literary works and idioms (**twixt** the devil and the deep blue sea = idiom meaning caught between two equally unappealing alternatives).

Nowadays the word **between** is more commonly used instead.

Categories

Place

I was **twixt** the devil and the deep blue sea.
Twixt a rock and a hard place.

Note: Both of the sample sentences are idioms and they both mean the speaker is facing unpalatable choices or decisions.

Notes

UNDER

In, at or to a lower position

Use this preposition:

To state that something is at a lower level than something else (Liverpool is **under** Chelsea in the league table).

To be subordinate to (The regiment is **under** the command of a colonel).

To be subject to (The city is **under** curfew since the riots).

To describe a reason (The bridge collapsed **under** the stress).

To move below a surface (The submarine slipped **under** the waves).

To be forced to do something because of unpleasant alternatives (The criminal started talking **under** the threat of a lifetime in prison).

To be less than (The price offer was **under** what I had paid for it).

There are also adverb, adjective and prefix versions of this word.

Categories

Direction

Put your bags **under** your chair during the exam..

The channel tunnel goes **under** the English channel.

Place

The old mine workings lay **under** the village.

The homeless people live **under** the railway arches.

Cause

He has a lot of funds **under** his control.

We got a bonus as we brought the project in **under** the budget.

Content

The operation went **under** the name Spy-catcher.

The chair broke **under** Hannah's grossly excessive weight.

Manner

People born **under** certain star signs are said to have certain traits.

The apprentice worked **under** the control of the master craftsman.

Comparison

The boxer weighed in **under** his ideal weight.

Everything on display is **under** a dollar.

UNDERNEATH

Below and out of sight

This preposition differs from **beneath** in that when something is **beneath** it can still be seen while **underneath** generally refers to something that is totally covered and cannot be seen.

It can be used:

To talk about being under the control of (It is difficult living a normal life **underneath** the constant surveillance of the state).

To be under the power of (the family knew they were **underneath** their grandmother in terms of priorities).

To be at a lower unseen place (the paper was buried **underneath** a pile of books).

To have moved below and out of sight – use the word **beneath** if it is still in sight (the damaged ship has sunk **underneath** the waves).

To be moving in a lower position (the floodwater was flowing quickly **underneath** the bridge).

It can be replaced with the words **below** or **beneath** when the subject can still be seen when the action is taking place.

There are adverb (She is spiteful **underneath**) and noun (The top was light whereas the **underneath** was dark) versions of this word.

Categories

Place

The metro was built **underneath** the city.
You'll find the pen **underneath** that pile of books.

Manner

He is a big softy **underneath** his gruff exterior.
She wears daring underwear **underneath** her modest business clothes.

Notes

UNLIKE

Different from *or* not typical of

This preposition is primarily used for comparisons of dissimilar things.

It can be used:

To state that something is in contrast to (He is tall **unlike** his brother who is short)

To state that something or someone is not the same as (He loves parties **unlike** his wife).

To be acting out of character (She is angry **unlike** her normal calm manner)

To behave in a different way (The journey was very quick **unlike** previous trips there).

In can be replaced with **different from** or **in comparison to**.

There is a new verb (She **unliked** him on Facebook) and an adjective (the twins were very **unlike**) versions of this word.

Categories

Comparison

She was neat and tidy **unlike** her brother.
The food this time was terrible **unlike** the last time.

Manner

It's **unlike** her to be quite so forceful.
It is **unlike** him to be late.

Notes

UNTIL

Do something until an end point is reached

This preposition is mainly used to **describe an action that will continue and will only stop when a predetermined endpoint, either in time or place, is reached.**

It is used:

To say up to the time of (We will keep working **until** 5 p.m.)

To state up to a relative point (The project team will be kept intact **until** the project is launched).

To say that at a certain point a change must be made (Keep going **until** the crossroads then turn left).

To continue no further than (Keep going **until** you reach the junction).

In speech it is often pronounced as 'till' (see the entry for till earlier in this section) – it can also be written as **till** or **'til**, particularly in fictional writing.

For situations involving time it can be replaced with **by the time that** or when giving directions by **when you reach**.

This word can also be used as a conjunction (I kept digging the garden **until** I couldn't see any more).

Categories

Time

I was up **until** 2 a.m.
We had to wait **until** the bell rang before we could leave the classroom.

Direction

Keep going straight **until** you get to the traffic lights then turn right.
Stay on the bus **until** it reaches the terminus.

Notes

UNTO

To a certain point and not beyond

This preposition is considered archaic, meaning it isn't used any more except in literature or in liturgical texts. It could still be used as it serves the purpose of stating that an action will continue until a particular goal is reached and no further. Plus, it is lovely word and should be revived.

It can be used:

To state that once a goal is reached the action will stop (He walked **unto** the church).

To state who is being provided with something (He preached **unto** the crowd).

To be concerned with ones self (He is a law **unto** himself - idiom meaning he does what he wants without a concern for others).

In can be replaced with **up to.**

Categories

Direction

The tribute was given **unto** the King.
Render **unto** Caesar that which is Caesar's. (Biblical reference)

Place

He came **unto** the hotel and sought a place to spend the night.
She drove **unto** her final destination.

Notes

　　　　Website: www.englishbook.shop

UP TO

To go as far as

This compound preposition can be used:

To state a point that is close to (I drove **up to** the barrier and then stopped).

To state a final place (I read the book **up to** the final chapter).

To enquire about or state a capability (Are you **up to** lifting that?).

To enquire about or state readiness (Are you **up to** trying again?).

To set a limit (I will need **up to** 20 copies of this book for my students).

To be incumbent upon (It is **up to** the prosecution to prove the charges).

To state that the decision rests elsewhere* (It's **up to** you whether we go out to eat).

To state the largest number (Up to 200,000 people attended the concert).

It can be replaced by **as far as** when referring to a particular place or **as many as** when referring to a particular amount.

*Note: It could be considered impolite saying "It's up to you" when stating that someone else should make the decision as it implies disinterest. It is preferable to say "It's your choice" instead.

Categories

Time

I stay **up to** 11 p.m. Most nights.
Do you want to work **up to** the time the bus leaves?.

Place

She liked to bathe in Asses' milk **up to** her chin.
We drove **up to** the store just before it closed.

Content

The stadium can hold **up to** 20,000 people.
I can put **up to** 10 gallons of fuel in my car.

UP

At or towards a higher position

This commonly used preposition is mainly used to **describe something, or someone, that is moving towards a higher position** (She is going **up** through the corporate ranks).

When giving directions the word **up** is often used to mean **going from one end of a street to the other even if the street itself is flat** (Go **up** the street to the end and my house is on the left).

It is also used when **discussing going to a [possibly] higher class** (She is going up in hierarchy) and **to describe going to a place, or area, where there are entertainment opportunities** (We went **up** the west end to a nightclub); whereas, **down**, is often **used to describe shopping, government or business area**s (We went **down** town to buy our groceries).

When it is used to describe a static position it is often paired with the preposition **above** (It is there, **up above** your head).

It is commonly used in phrasal verbs - with verbs that talk about movement (for example with: go, put, get, move, look, wake and look).

It has no direct preposition replacement.

There are adjective, (What's **up**? – idiomatic meaning: what's wrong *or* what do you want), adverb (You must all stand **up** when the teacher comes into the room), noun (He's on the **up** - UK: meaning honest), verb (They **upped** the price of cooking oil by 50% overnight.) and prefix – used to mean higher or improved (examples; **up**scale, **up**stream or **up**-market.) versions of this word.

Categories

Direction

Go **up** the stairs to the third floor and the office is in front of you.
You need to go **up** the high street and turn left at the top.

Place

The towpath goes **up** the side of the canal. (along)
We went **up** the side of the mountain.

Comparison

The temperature went **up** the scale quickly.
He drove **up** the street quicker than I would dare to.

                    Website: www.englishbook.shop

UPON

Above and in contact with *or* supported by

This preposition can be used:

To describe being supported by something else (She relies **upon** him for emotional support)

To be at the highest most point of something (the country's flag was placed **upon** the mountaintop).

To be at a specific moment in time (**Upon** the third stroke it will be 12 o clocked precisely).

To wear on the head (I put the **upon** my head).

To describe an experience (I had fun **upon** my holiday).

To describe an imminent event (The holidays will soon be **upon** us).

This preposition is similar to '**on**' and they can generally be used interchangeably; however, '**upon**' is generally regarded as the more formal version (I placed it **upon** the table). On the other hand, '**on**' is more commonly used in speech.

It may also be replaced with **supported by** when discussing who is providing for someone else's needs.

There is an adverb version of this word, which is often used in phrasal verbs, meaning to be the target of an action (He was set **upon** by a pack of dogs).

It can also be used in the idiomatic phrasal verb, **put upon**, meaning to be taken advantage of (I feel **put upon** by the way he treats me).

Categories

Direction

Please register at the reception **upon** arrival.
You'll need to fill out an immigration card **upon** arrival.

Place

At the coronation, a crown was placed **upon** the King's head.
There is a stand on trees **upon** the hillside.

Time

Once **upon** a time.
Emphasis is placed **upon** good timekeeping.

UPWARDS OF

Over a stated amount

This preposition is sometimes regarded as an adjective by some grammar books and dictionaries.

It has been included in the preposition list as the number that follows it should be regarded as a determiner rather than another adjective.

Its main use is **for estimating a number that will probably be higher** (We are expecting **upwards of** ten guests at the party).

In the US it is written as **upward of**.

Categories

Content

Upwards of 50,000 people were at the concert.
I want to earn **upwards of** $100,000 a year.

Time

It'll take **upwards of** 3 hours to sail across the lake.
The plane took **upwards of** ten hours to reach its destination.

Notes

UPTIL/UPTILL

During the time before *or* to a specific higher place

This preposition is generally regarded as being obsolete; however, it serves as a simplified version of the compound prepositions **up until** or **up till**.

It can be used:

To indicate a period before (Uptill then, everything was going well).

To go from one high place to a higher place (You need to keep filling the tank **uptill** the maximum mark has been reached).

It can be replaced with **until**.

Categories

Content

You can only keep putting things in it **uptill** that point is reached).
His wages increased annually **uptill** he reached $100,000 a year.

Time

I will stay at work **uptill** the traffic dies down.
She waited **uptill** her friend arrived.

Notes

VERSUS

Comparative choices *or* against

This preposition, which is often abbreviated as: **v**, **vs** or **-v-**, can be used:

To state something that is against (It looks like you **versus** me then).

To be in opposition to (The match tonight is the Russian boxer **versus** the African one)

To be compared to (I am not sure which has the most sugar when comparing coke **versus** red bull).

To identify the opposing participants in a legal action (The case was known as Arkell **versus** Pressdram).

It is generally regarded as more intense than against; so, if you want to add emphasis to a particular match between, say, old rivals, or bitter opponents in a court case, then use **versus**. In general use the word **against** can be used instead.

Categories

Comparison

My choice of car comes down to Toyota **versus** Honda
He had to the choice of private **versus** public healthcare for his operation

Content

The match tonight is Manchester United **versus** Arsenal
Abortion was legalized in the US following Wade **versus** Rowe.

Notes

VIA

Through *or* the method used

This preposition is used:

To state a key point on a route (We drove to Dover **via** the M20 motorway).

To pass through (I like to go to work **via** the park).

To show what was used to achieve a result (We were able to get a discount **via** our membership card).

To show the medium used to achieve something (He let everyone know about the concert **via** his website).

This word may be replaced with **through** or **by way of.**

Categories

Direction

You can connect it to the computer **via** the USB port.
The flight to London goes **via** Singapore.

Content

Irregular verbs came to us primarily **via** the Anglo Saxons.
He delivered his report **via** the medium of French.

Notes

VICE

Instead of *or* in place of

This proposition is used:

To suggest an option (You can have this Mercedes **vice** the Toyota you booked to hire).

To be instead of (The new boss will be Fred **vice** Bert who was expected to take over).

Vice versa is a commonly used collocation and is generally regarded as an adverb: meaning true in the opposite order or either way (You can go first and I can follow or **vice** versa).

It can be replaced with **instead of**.

There are adjective (He is the **vice** president – meaning 2nd in command to) and noun (He has many **vices** - Moral weaknesses) versions of this word.

Categories

Comparison

I used a hammer **vice** the proper tool
We will go ahead with the original plan **vice** any better suggestions.

Notes

VIS-À-VIS

In relation to

This preposition is used:

To state relative positions or stances (The US's position was relaxed **vis-à-vis** the EU's more hard-line stance).

To give comparisons (How does this quote compare **vis-à-vis** the others we received?).

To be opposite from (His viewpoint **vis-à-vis** mine could not be more different).

To be across from (He was seated **vis-à-vis** the ambassador).

To set facing (The portrait was hung **vis-à-vis** the entrance).

It can be replaced with **in relation to** in most instances.

This word was derived from French and so the a is usually accented (à).

It is sometimes written as **viz-a-viz**.

Categories

Comparison

Should the decisions be made locally or centrally **vis-à-vis** local issues?
There was some discussion **vis-à-vis** the EU's role in Africa.

Content

We need to talk **vis-à-vis** these proposed sales targets.
The countries met the criteria **vis-à-vis** nuclear disarmament.

Notes

WITH

Presence, opposition, agreement *or* togetherness

This common preposition is used:

To talk about being in the company of (I went **with** my wife to the cinema).

To be alongside (Will you walk **with** me?)

To start to date (Will you go out **with** me?)

To state similar things being together (The aircraft carrier sailed **with** a destroyer escort).

To be close to (I prefer to keep my bag **with** me).

To be near to (She walked arm in arm **with** her boyfriend).

To follow closely (He walked out **with** the rest of his class).

To be against (He had a huge argument **with** his wife).

To be in support of (The crowd were all **with** the speaker).

To suggest an addition (Would you like some milk **with** your tea?).

To be an accessory to (He committed the robbery **with** two accomplices).

To describe an addition (I loved the ice cream **with** the cherry on top).

To describe a simultaneous state (It exploded **with** a huge roar).

To describe events that happened in immediate succession (There was one large explosion **with** a series of smaller ones afterwards).

To describe an additional effect (The earthquake caused huge damage **with** the possibility of further building collapses).

To be a consequence of (You will get nowhere **with** that attitude).

To be in support of (I am **with** you in this campaign).

To have interactions with (She agreed to play tennis **with** me).

To state the means by which something was done (He was murdered **with** a knife).

To have an inclusion (Buy our cornflakes **with** added niacin).

This preposition can be used for both agreement (I agreed **with** her) and disagreement (I argued **with** her).

WITH

Categories

Direction

You can come **with** me as I'm going there.
The yachtsman hoped the wind was **with** him today.

Place

I love walking in the countryside **with** nature all around me.
He liked being outside **with** his dog.

Cause

She cried **with** the pain.
I fixed it **with** superglue.

Content

I like cream **with** my coffee.
She is tall **with** blond hair.

Manner

She is so argumentative no-one like to be **with** her.
He walks **with** an almost military precision.

Comparison

You can either pay cash or **with** instalments of $10 per month.
Does this handbag go **with** these shoes?

Time

He looked more distinguished **with** age.
Winter is gloomier **with** shorter days.

Notes

Reference

WITHIN

Inside an area *or* before a specified duration ends

This preposition is used;

To indicate inclusion within the scope of (It was not **within** the power of the court to order his continued detention)

To define a point before a specified duration ends (You must finish the test **within** the time allotted).

To indicate spatial enclosure (The prisoners were kept **within** their cells for 23 hours a day).

To be constrained by (I am stuck **within** these four walls all day).

To define a container (She kept a lot of strange things **within** her handbag).

It can also be used **to talk about actions taking place inside defined boundaries** (A lot of activities took place **within** the sports complex).

It can be replaced with **inside** when referring to being in an enclosed space. **Within** is often used to talk more about the enclosure; whereas, **inside** refers to where the things/people are (The convicts were housed **within** the prison walls - The convicts were **inside** the prison). When used for time, **within**, generally means that the time being was set by someone onto the person doing it, while **inside** refers to an achievement by the person doing it (You need to complete one circuit of the track **within** 3 minutes to qualify - He managed to complete one circuit of the track **inside** 1.26 minutes)

Categories

Place

Many people like to live **within** sight of the sea.
You cannot build a house **within** the boundaries of a national park.

Time

Can you get this done **within** the timescale?
I need this typing up **within** the hour.

Content

The job is well **within** his capabilities.
The project has to be done **within** the allocated budget.

WITHOUT

Not doing something *or* lacking something

Use this preposition:

To specify not wanting to have something (I'd prefer to go **without** her)

To admit to not having used something/someone to do something (I did everything **without** any help from him).

To describe not being in possession of (I went out **without** my umbrella).

To describe a negative characteristic of someone/something (He goes through life **without** a clue).

To be outside of – old use (It was cold **without** the house).

There is a very similar preposition, **outwith**, which means beyond or outside of.

In most cases it can be replaced with **excluding.**

There is an adverb version of this word (If you don't like it you can go **without**).

Categories

Content

I'm hungry as I went **without** breakfast.
You can't get into the club **without** a tie.

Manner

She is not confident **without** her make up.
He is not **without** his good points.

Comparison

What is the price **without** the purchase tax?
The version **without** the turbo is slightly cheaper.

Notes

ENGLISHBOOK.SHOP
Where you come to learn

The free companion website provides a number of useful tools. One of the most useful tools is the custom search facility. This tool allows you to type in, say, a verb structure, together with other keywords, and it then searches a number of high quality, international publications and newspapers to match your criteria. In the example below the verb structure "have been used" (note the "speech marks") together with the keyword "computers".

Phrase Search - enter a phrase in "commas" to see it in use

"have been used" + "computers"

Clicking the search button opened a pop up window on which the first entry was:

Are programs better than people at predicting reoffending ...

https://www.economist.com/.../are-programs-better-than-people-at-predicting-reoffending

Jan 17, 2018 ... IN AMERICA, computers have been used to assist bail and :

Clicking on the link brought up the full article so the reference can be seen in the context in which it is used. The resulting paragraph looked like this:

IN AMERICA, computers have been used to assist bail and sentencing decisions for many years. Their proponents argue that the rigorous logic of an algorithm, trained with a vast amount of data, can make judgments about whether a convict will reoffend that are unclouded by human bias.

Source: The Economist - The full article can be found at:
https://www.economist.com/science-and-technology/2018/01/17/are-programs-better-than-people-at-predicting-reoffending

Using this tool and the dictionary on the site, you can search for any combination of tense structures and keywords to give you ideas on how you can structure your own sentences based on the results and the CORE colours. The website can be reached by using the QR code or the URL on the bottom of the page.

PREPOSITION WORKSHEETS

The following worksheets are designed to allow you to create your own sentences based on the prepositions listed on the left of the table. The prepositions below are used for highlighting times or time periods. Other preposition types are on subsequent pages.

Your Name:

Prep.	Your Sentences
at	
on	
in	
for	
since	
during	
before	
after	
by	
until (or till)	
from… until	
up to	

PREPOSITIONS OF PLACE

Prep.	Your Sentences
around	
at	
from	
in	
inside	
on	
outside	
past	
through	
to	
towards	
beneath	
underneath	
under	
on	
in	
by	
at	
to	

Website: www.englishbook.shop

GENERAL PREPOSITIONS

Preposition	Your Sentences
about	
above	
according to	
across	
after	
against	
along	
amidst	
amongst	
around	
at	
because of	
before	
behind	
below	

GENERAL PREPOSITIONS

Preposition	Your Sentences
beneath	
beside	
between	
beyond	
but	
by	
concerning	
down	
during	
except	
for	
from	
in	
in spite of	
inside	

     Website: www.englishbook.shop

GENERAL PREPOSITIONS

Preposition	Your Sentences
instead of	
into	
like	
near	
of	
off	
on	
onto	
out	
out of	
outside	
over	
past	
regarding	
since	

GENERAL PREPOSITIONS

Preposition	Your Sentences
through	
throughout	
to	
towards	
under	
underneath	
until	
up	
upon	
with	
within	
without	

Teacher's Comments

PREPOSITION SELECTOR

In this section you can select the ideal preposition to suit the context of your writing.

ABOUT   ABOVE   ABSENT

ALIAS   ALONG   ANTI

BAR   BEFORE   BELOW

FOR   FROM   GIVEN

INSIDE   INTO   LESS

MINUS   NEAR   OF

ONTO   OUT   OVER

PER   **PLUS**   POST

RE   ROUND   SANS

SINCE   THAN   TILL

TWIXT   UNDER   UNLIKE

UP TO   UP   UPON

VIA   VICE   WITH

Selector

A

Website: www.englishbook.shop

C

D

Selector

Selector

Selector

Selector

Website: www.englishbook.shop

O

Selector

Selector

Selector

Website: www.englishbook.shop

9 781916 075719